The Low-Fat Kroger Cookbook

*Budget your fat and finances
with easy recipes and Kroger brands!*

by
Karen McNamara
and
Michelle Lombardo, D.C.

WELLNESS INCORPORATED

ISBN 0-9648438-1-1

Printed in the United States of America

Hardy Heart™ and Don't Gamble With Your Health® are registered trademarks
of Wellness Incorporated.

Illustrations by Mark Herron

Contents

Foreword

Thank you for buying this valuable tool for healthier living. We hope you and your family enjoy these simple, delicious recipes while simultaneously keeping within your budget. To inspire you to make the healthy eating changes such as limiting your fat intake and increasing your fiber intake, we encourage you to read the following excerpt from Dr. Lombardo's *Don't Gamble With Your Health* book.

"I personally was astounded by a fact that should literally scare all of us into changing some of our habits today: 50% of the people who have a fatal heart attack had no prior symptoms. The heart attack was the first sign that there was anything wrong."

"The good news is there are a few habits that are common factors in most of the disease processes. Consequently, modification or elimination of these habits is a major step toward possible avoidance of many diseases. So you don't have to do 30 different things to prevent 30 different diseases. You can go to regular stores and eat normal foods and lose the fat while eating satisfying quantities of food. Low-fat, high-fiber eating is the best thing you can do for yourself and your family today for a better quality of life in years to come."

This cookbook was designed with the busy person in mind. If you don't have time to prepare 7-course meals but still want to eat well, your search is over! This cookbook is set up the way you eat throughout your day.

When time permits, enjoy a healthy low-fat breakfast. On those busy mornings when the entire family is rushing to get the day going grab a "no-time-to-cook breakfast."

Look forward to lunch time with these good tasting, good for you, recipe suggestions. Before tossing those high-fat snacks into the lunchbox or bag, take a second to look at some great tasting, low-fat alternatives listed and pictured in the "Lunch Box Snacks for Kids of All Ages" section.

Dinner time already? If you have less than 30 minutes until the flood gates open and your hungry family charges to the kitchen table—no sweat! Pick a quick recipe from the main dish section and before you know it . . . dinner is served.

For each main meal, choose a vegetable, rice or potato, and a bread side dish. Many of these dishes can be prepared ahead of time.

If you are entertaining guests or going to a "BYOHD" (bring your own hors d'oeuvres) party, try one of the delicious appetizer recipes. Because they taste so good, no one will ever suspect they are low-fat. Keep it a secret and you'll be anonymously contributing to a healthier society!

At the end of each recipe notice there are two serving sizes: the regular and the "hardy" size. The "hardy" size is for athletes, men, growing boys, anyone with a fast metabolism or in case you want to serve one of the side dishes as a main meal.

Try modifying any of these recipes to suit your taste. Remember spices are fat-free and add a wealth of flavor to any dish. Also be sure to check out the label to learn the fat content before adding any ingredient.

To sharpen your label reading skills, turn to the next page for some simple explanations of nutritional information.

You will notice illustrations of a heart throughout the cookbook and next to the "Hardy Size" information. Hardy Heart™ is one of the characters in our children's wellness program, *The OrganWise Guys™.* Since taking care of your heart is so vital to good health (and low-fat eating is one of the major ways to be "heart smart"), Hardy Heart serves as a constant reminder throughout the cookbook.

Finally, be on the lookout for a wonderful variety of new Kroger products that will assist you in continuing to "budget your fat and finances" while eating delicious food. Enjoy!

—*Karen McNamara*

NUTRITION FACTS Ⓐ

In 1994, new food labeling regulations by the FDA (Food & Drug Administration) required nearly all foods in your supermarket to carry the new food label. It's called Nutrition Facts. Foods which do not provide significant nutrients, like coffee, tea, spices and bottled water, are not required to carry the new Nutrition Facts label.

INFORMATION REQUIRED Ⓑ

All of this information about serving size and specific nutrients are required to be on the food label.

SODIUM

You call it "salt" and the label calls it "sodium." Either way, it may lead to high blood pressure in some people. Try to have less than 2,400 milligrams of sodium every day.

Nutrition Facts Ⓐ

Serving Size: 1/2 cup (114g)
Servings Per Container: 4

Amount Per Serving

Calories 90   Calories from Fat 30

	% Daily Values*
Total Fat 3g	5%
Saturated Fat 0g	0%
Cholesterol 0g	0%
Sodium 300mg	13%
Total Carbohydrate 13g	4%
Dietary Fiber 3g	12%
Sugars 3g	

Protein 3g

Vitamin A	80%	•	Vitamin C	60%
Calcium	4%	•	Iron	4%

* Percent Daily Values are based on a 2,000 calorie diet. Your daily values may be higher or lower depending on your calorie needs:

	Calories	2,000	2,500
Total Fat	Less than	65g	80g
Sat Fat	Less than	20g	25g
Cholesterol	Less than	300mg	300mg
Sodium	Less than	2,400mg	2,400mg
Total Carbohydrate		300g	375g
Fiber		25g	30g

Source: How to Read the New Food Label
American Heart Association and Food and Drug Administration   Ⓒ

CARBOHYDRATE

Carbohydrates are found in breads, cereals, grains, pastas, fruits and vegetables. Choose more of these foods, they provide the energy your body needs along with valuable nutrients.

FIBER

Fruits, vegetables, whole grain foods and dried beans are all good sources of fiber. Try to eat at least 25 grams of fiber daily.

VITAMINS & MINERALS

Only two vitamins, A and C, and two minerals, calcium and iron, are required on the food label. A food company can list other vitamins and minerals in the food. Your goal is to eat a combination of foods that will add up to 100% of each of these nutrients.

SERVING SIZE

Similar food products now have comparable serving sizes. Serving sizes are based upon amounts people customarily eat. However, serving sizes of foods packaged in single serving containers may vary.

% DAILY VALUES

% Daily Values show how a food fits into a 2,000 calorie reference diet. You can use % Daily Values to compare foods and see how the amount of a nutrient in a serving of food fits in a 2,000 calorie reference diet.

FAT

Most people need to watch fat intake. The Nutrition Facts label helps you accomplish this by listing the total grams of fat, the amount of calories coming from fat and the percent Daily Value provided by a serving. Saturated fat is part of the total fat in a food, but it is listed separately because of its association with increasing blood cholesterol levels and the risk of heart disease.

CHOLESTEROL

Cholesterol is a fat-like substance. Try to eat less than 300 milligrams of cholesterol each day. You'll find cholesterol only in animal foods: meat, poultry, fish, eggs, and dairy foods.

DAILY VALUES ⊕

Daily Values are the new label reference numbers. These numbers are based on current nutrition recommendations established by the National Academy of Sciences.

Some labels list the daily values for a daily diet of 2,000 and 2,500 calories. Your own nutrient needs may be less than or more than the Daily Values on the label.

Authors' note: *The above information has been taken from the brochure, "Food Label Facts" developed for Kroger by Kim Galeaz, a registered dietian and consultant.*

Breakfasts

The most important meal of the day!

Colorful Egg White Omelet

GROCERY LIST:

 **Brand**

Other Items:
scallions
green or red pepper

RECIPE INGREDIENTS:

3 Kroger eggs (whites only)

1 tablespoon scallions (sliced)

2 tablespoons diced green or red pepper

1 tablespoon Kroger Lite Classics Shredded Cheddar Cheese

2 large Kroger Black Olives (sliced)

Lite salt & Kroger Pepper to taste (optional)

Kroger Buttery Cooking Spray

DIRECTIONS:

Combine scallions, peppers, and olives in a small bowl.

Separate egg yolks from whites and save whites in a bowl.

Over medium heat use a small skillet sprayed with cooking spray. Pour egg whites into heated pan. Sprinkle vegetables on top of egg whites. Add lite salt and pepper (optional). Cover and cook for approximately 4 minutes. Add cheese and replace cover for 30–45 seconds until cheese is melted.

Makes one omelet.

SIDE DISH RECOMMENDATIONS:

- Kroger Orange Juice
- Cut-up fruit
- Kroger Vitamins
- Kroger Multi-Grain Bread, toasted, with jelly

SERVING SIZE & NUTRITIONAL INFORMATION:

Serving Size:
  1 omelet

Calories: 91

Total Fat: 2.25 g

Fiber: .4 g

Sodium: 264 mg

Cholesterol: 3.75 mg

Carbohydrates: 2.6 g

Protein: 13 g

Hardy Size:
  2 omelets

Calories: 182

Total Fat: 4.5 g

Fiber: .8 g

Sodium: 528 mg

Cholesterol: 7.5 mg

Carbohydrates: 5.2 g

Protein: 26 g

Egg & Cheese Muffin

GROCERY LIST:

 **Brands**

INGREDIENTS:

½ cup Kroger Egg Substitute

1 Kroger English Muffin

1 Kroger Fat-Free Cheese Single

Dash Kroger Pepper (optional)

Dash salt (optional)

Kroger Canola Cooking Spray

DIRECTIONS:

Spray frying pan with cooking spray. Cook eggs scrambled style. Add salt and pepper if desired.

Toast English muffin.

On half of muffin, top with egg and then cheese. Top with other muffin half.

Dip in ketchup for more flavor.

Yields one muffin.

SIDE DISH RECOMMENDATIONS:

- Kroger Blend O' Five Juice
- Kroger Vitamins

SERVING SIZE & NUTRITIONAL INFORMATION:

Serving Size:
  1 egg muffin

Calories: 215

Total Fat: .5 g

Fiber: 2 g

Sodium: 660 mg

Cholesterol: 0

Carbohydrates: 29 g

Protein: 21 g

Hardy Size:
  2 egg muffins

Calories: 430

Total Fat: 1 g

Fiber: 4 g

Sodium: 1320 mg

Cholesterol: 0

Carbohydrates: 58 g

Protein: 42 g

French Toast

GROCERY LIST:

 **Brands**

Economical &
Delicious, too!

INGREDIENTS:

1 cup Kroger Egg Substitute

1 cup Kroger A/B Plus ½% Milk

2 teaspoon Kroger Cinnamon

8 slices Kroger Multi-Grain Bread

Kroger Buttery Cooking Spray

Kroger Butter Sprinkles

Kroger Lite Syrup

DIRECTIONS:

In a large mixing bowl combine egg substitute, milk, and cinnamon.

Heat up pan that has been coated with cooking spray.

Dip 4 pieces of bread in egg mixture and place side by side in pan. Cook on both sides until toasted. Repeat until all bread is cooked.

Serve with ¾ teaspoon butter sprinkles and approximately ¼ cup of syrup per serving.

Yields 4 servings.

Variation: Use Kroger Powdered Sugar instead of syrup.

SIDE DISH RECOMMENDATIONS:

- Scrambled Kroger Break-Free Egg Substitutes
- Kroger Orange Juice
- Kroger Vitamins

SERVING SIZE & NUTRITIONAL INFORMATION:

Serving Size:
  2 French toasts
	Hardy Size:
	  4 French toasts

Calories: 300	Calories: 600
Total Fat: 1.3 g	Total Fat: 2.6 g
Fiber: 2.3 g	Fiber: 4.6 g
Sodium: 660 mg	Sodium: 1320 mg
Cholesterol: <5 mg	Cholesterol: <5 mg
Carbohydrates: 56 g	Carbohydrates: 112 g
Protein: 14 g	Protein: 28 g

Ham, Egg & Cheese Casserole

GROCERY LIST:

 **Brands**

Other Items:
Optional items: onion,
green pepper, garlic powder

INGREDIENTS:

6 slices Kroger Multi-Grain Bread

1 package Kroger Lite Classics Shredded Cheddar Cheese

6 slices Kroger Country Club 98% Fat-Free Cooked Ham

2 cups Kroger Egg Substitute

1 ¼ cups Kroger A/B Plus ½% Milk

¼ teaspoon Kroger Pepper

Kroger Canola Cooking Spray

Optional items: ¼ cup diced onion

¼ cup diced green pepper

¼ teaspoon garlic powder

DIRECTIONS:

Spray 9 x 13 inch baking dish with non-stick spray.

Lay 6 bread slices side by side covering bottom of dish.

Sprinkle package of cheese evenly in layer on top of bread. Cut six slices of ham into 1 inch squares. Separate and layer evenly on top of cheese. (If using onion or green pepper, layer it on top of ham.)

In a mixing bowl combine egg substitute, milk, pepper, and optional garlic powder. Whip thoroughly with fork. Pour this mixture over layered items in baking dish. Let sit for 10 minutes while oven is preheating to 375°.

Bake for 50–55 minutes until done.

SIDE DISH RECOMMENDATIONS:

- Kroger English Muffin with Kroger Jelly
- Cantaloupe
- Kroger Vitamins

SERVING SIZE & NUTRITIONAL INFORMATION:

Serving Size:
  $\frac{1}{12}$ of casserole

Calories: 117

Total Fat: 2.6 g

Fiber: .5 g

Sodium: 325 mg

Cholesterol: 88 mg

Carbohydrates: 9 g

Protein: 13.3

Hardy Size:
  $\frac{1}{9}$ of casserole

Calories: 156

Total Fat: 3.5 g

Fiber: .6 g

Sodium: 434 mg

Cholesterol: 117 mg

Carbohydrates: 12 g

Protein: 18 g

Pancakes and Scrambled Eggs

GROCERY LIST:

 Brands

INGREDIENTS:

Kroger Original Pancake and Waffle Mix

Kroger Canola Cooking Spray

½ cup Kroger Egg Substitute (per person)

Kroger Pepper

Lite Salt (optional)

¼ cup Kroger Lite Syrup (per 2 pancake serving)

¾ teaspoon Kroger Butter Sprinkles (per 2 pancakes)

DIRECTIONS:

Follow directions on pancake mix box for desired quantities of pancakes.

After pancakes are done spray more non-stick spray on skillet. Pour in ½ cup of egg substitute per person. Add salt and pepper if desired. Cook eggs stirring occasionally until done.

Serve pancakes with ¾ teaspoon butter sprinkles and ¼ cup syrup per serving.

SIDE DISH RECOMMENDATIONS:

- Kroger Orange Juice
- Low-fat turkey bacon (any brand)
- Kroger Vitamins

SERVING SIZE & NUTRITIONAL INFORMATION:

Serving Size:
   2 pancakes & ½ cup
   scrambled eggs

Calories: 316

Total Fat: 2 g

Fiber: <1 g

Sodium: 1010 mg

Cholesterol: 10 mg

Carbohydrates: 53 g

Protein: 16 g

Hardy Size:
   4 pancakes & 1 cup
   scrambled eggs

Calories: 632

Total Fat: 4 g

Fiber: 1 g

Sodium: 2020 mg

Cholesterol: 20 mg

Carbohydrates: 106 g

Protein: 32 g

No-Time-To-Cook Breakfasts

If your mornings are hectic, make sure you grab one of these quick, healthy starters.

Daily Vitamins

DIRECTIONS:

To get the most benefit from vitamins, take them in conjunction with food. Whether you are eating on the run or having a full, balanced breakfast, take your vitamins to ensure you meet the daily requirements.

98% Fat-Free Muffin & Blend O'Five Juice

Serving Size:
   1 muffin &
   1 cup juice
Calories: 320
Total Fat: .5 g
 Fiber: 4 g
Sodium: 370 mg
Cholesterol: 0 mg
Carbohydrates: 76 g
Protein: 7 g

DIRECTIONS:

98% fat-free muffins are in the deli section. They can be eaten cold or warm. The juice is loaded with vitamins.

Non-Fat Cottage Cheese & Banana

Serving Size:
  ½ cup cottage cheese
  & one medium banana
Calories: 175
Total Fat: .6 g
Fiber: 3 g
Sodium: 421 mg
Cholesterol: 10 mg
Carbohydrates: 32 g
Protein: 14 g

DIRECTIONS:

Slice banana and mix with cottage cheese.

Instant Oatmeal & Orange Juice

Serving Size:
  1 pouch oatmeal &
  1 cup orange juice
Calories: 240
Total Fat: 2 g
Fiber: 3 g
Sodium: 105 mg
Cholesterol: 0 mg
Carbohydrates: 49 g
Protein: 6 g

DIRECTIONS:

Follow directions on assorted instant oatmeal box. Have one cup of the 100% orange juice for a good dose of vitamin C.

Low-Fat Yogurt & Granola Cereal

Serving Size:
   1 yogurt &
   ¼ cup granola
Calories: 265
Total Fat: 1.5 g
Fiber: 1.5 g
Sodium: 120 mg
Cholesterol: 0 mg
Carbohydrates: 53 g
Protein: 9.5 g

DIRECTIONS:

Combine any variety of Healthy Indulgence Yogurt with Kroger Low-Fat Granola Cereal. Enjoy.

English Muffin, Cream Cheese & Jelly

Serving Size:
   1 muffin, 2 T cream
   cheese, & 1 T Jelly
Calories: 210
Total Fat: .5 g
Fiber: 2.5 g
Sodium: 380 mg
Cholesterol: <5 mg
Carbohydrates: 40 g
Protein: 9 g

DIRECTIONS:

Split Kroger English Muffin in half and toast until golden brown. Spread Kroger Fat-Free Cream Cheese on each half and then your favorite Kroger Fruit Preserve.

Raisin Bran Cereal & Low-Fat Milk

Serving Size:
  1 cup cereal &
  1 cup A/B plus milk
Calories: 270
Total Fat: 2 g
Fiber: 7 g
Sodium: 380 mg
Cholesterol: < 5 mg
Carbohydrates: 55 g
Protein: 13 g

DIRECTIONS:

In a bowl combine raisin bran (or any high-fiber Kroger cereal) with Kroger A/B Plus low-fat milk. This milk has aci-dophilos and other live cultures for a healthy colon.

Bagel & Fat-Free Cream Cheese

Serving Size:
  1 Bagel & 4 T of
  cream cheese
Calories: 280
Total Fat: 2 g
Fiber: 2 g
Sodium: 690 mg
Cholesterol: <25 mg
Carbohydrates: 49 g
Protein: 16 g

DIRECTIONS:

Split open (any variety) Kroger bagel from the deli section. Toast if desired, and load with Kroger Fat-Free Cream Cheese.

Quick Pick Cereal

GROCERY LIST:

 **Brands**

Serving Size:
  ¾ – 1 cup (cereal only)
Calories: 100 – 120
Fat: 0 – 2 g
Fiber: 0 – 3 g
Sodium: 40 – 280 mg
(See each package for
  exact amount)

DIRECTIONS:

Pick one of the above cereals and use Kroger A/B Plus
½% milk. In addition to being low in fat , A (acidophilus)
& B (bacillus) are the good bacteria that promote a healthy
environment in the colon.

Lunches

Broccoli & Cheese Quiche

GROCERY LIST:

 **Brands**

Other Items:
small white onion

INGREDIENTS:

2 cups Kroger Frozen Fresh Chopped Broccoli

⅓ cup diced onion

1 cup Kroger Lite Classics Shredded Cheddar Cheese

2 cups Kroger Egg Substitute

¾ cup Kroger A/B Plus ½% Milk

2 tablespoons Kroger Flour

½ teaspoon Kroger Butter Sprinkles

¼ teaspoon Kroger Pepper

Kroger Canola Cooking Spray

DIRECTIONS:

Preheat oven to 375°.

Spray 9-inch pie tin with non-stick spray.

Place frozen broccoli, diced onion, and shredded cheese in pie tin. Mix and spread evenly. In another bowl combine: 2 cartons egg substitute, milk, flour, butter sprinkles, and pepper. Whip together with fork until thoroughly blended.

Pour over broccoli, onion, and cheese. Bake at 375° for 60–70 minutes or until done.

It is easy to make two by doubling the recipe.

SIDE DISH RECOMMENDATIONS:

• English Muffin or Roll

SERVING SIZE & NUTRITIONAL INFORMATION:

Serving Size:
  ⅛ of pie

Calories: 93

Total Fat: 2 g

Fiber: .5 g

Sodium: 184 mg

Cholesterol: 8 mg

Carbohydrates: 5 g

Protein: 12 g

Hardy Size:
  ¼ of pie

Calories: 186

Total Fat: 4 g

Fiber: 1 g

Sodium: 368 mg

Cholesterol: 16 mg

Carbohydrates: 10 g

Protein: 24 g

Grilled Cheese & Tomato Sandwich

GROCERY LIST:

 Brands

Other Items:
scallions
1 medium tomato

INGREDIENTS:

1 tablespoon scallions (chopped)

1 medium tomato (sliced)

6 slices Kroger Multi-Grain Bread

6 slices Kroger Fat-Free Cheese Singles

3 teaspoons Kroger Spicy Brown Mustard

Kroger Buttery Cooking Spray

Dash of Kroger Pepper (optional)

DIRECTIONS:

Chop scallions & slice tomato.

Heat medium sized skillet, sprayed with cooking spray. Take 3 bread slices; place 2 slices of cheese on each and top with ⅓ of the scallions, mustard, tomato, and dash of pepper. Top with remaining bread. Spray each outer side of bread with cooking spray and place a sandwich in skillet and cover.

Cook each side for approximately 3–4 minutes until bread is golden brown and cheese is melted.

Makes 3 sandwiches.

SIDE DISH RECOMMENDATIONS:

- Kroger Sensible Indulgence Fat-Free Potato Chips
- Kroger Dill Pickles

SERVING SIZE & NUTRITIONAL INFORMATION:

Serving Size:
   1 sandwich

Calories: 199

Total Fat: 1.1 g

Fiber: 2.4 g

Sodium: 923 mg

Cholesterol: 0

Carbohydrates: 36 mg

Protein: 14.5 g

Hardy Size:
   1 ½ sandwiches

Calories: 299

Total Fat: 1.7 g

Fiber: 3.7 g

Sodium: 1384 mg

Cholesterol: 0

Carbohydrates: 53 g

Protein: 22 g

Grilled Turkey Reuben

GROCERY LIST:

 **Brands**

Other Items:

head of cabbage or
pre-bagged coleslaw mix
sliced turkey breast
rye bread

INGREDIENTS:

3 cups shredded cabbage or coleslaw mix

1 tablespoon Kroger Lite Whipped Dressing

2 tablespoon Kroger Fat-Free Thousand Island Salad Dressing

12 slices rye bread

3 teaspoons Kroger Spicy Brown Mustard

6 slices Kroger Fat-Free Swiss Cheese

6 ounces sliced turkey breast (low-fat)

Kroger Buttery Cooking Spray

DIRECTIONS:

Thoroughly mix cabbage, thousand island dressing, and lite whipped dressing together.

Layer 6 bread slices with mustard, turkey, one slice of cheese, and cabbage mixture (evenly). Top them with the remaining bread slices.

Spray a heated skillet with cooking spray. Then spray each side of sandwich with cooking spray and place in skillet.

Cook each sandwich on medium heat 3–4 minutes on each side. Serve hot.

Yields 6 sandwiches.

SIDE DISH RECOMMENDATIONS:

- Kroger Dill Pickles
- Sensible Indulgence Potato Chips
- Kroger Fat-Free Pretzels

SERVING SIZE & NUTRITIONAL INFORMATION:

Serving Size:
  1 sandwich

Calories: 238

Total Fat: 3 g

Fiber: 3 g

Sodium: 1042 mg

Cholesterol: 9 mg

Carbohydrates: 35 g

Protein: 16 g

Hardy Size:
  2 sandwiches

Calories: 476

Total Fat: 6 g

Fiber: 6 g

Sodium: 2084 mg

Cholesterol: 18 mg

Carbohydrates: 70 mg

Protein: 32 g

Ham & Cheese Submarine Sandwich

GROCERY LIST:

 **Brands**

Other Items:
deli sub rolls
turkey (2 oz. per sandwich)
low-fat mayonnaise
tomato (optional)
lettuce (optional)

INGREDIENTS:

1 wheat bun (from deli)

2 slices Kroger Country Club 98% Fat-Free Cooked Ham

2 slices 98% fat-free turkey

2 slices Kroger Fat-Free Swiss Singles

1 tablespoon low-fat mayonnaise

1 teaspoon Kroger Fat-Free Zesty Italian Dressing

Mustard, sliced tomato, lettuce (optional)

DIRECTIONS:

Open wheat bun. Spread mayonnaise (and mustard, if desired) on top of bun.

Layer ham, turkey, and cheese on bottom half of bun.

Put optional items of lettuce and sliced tomatoes on top of cheese.

Sprinkle zesty Italian dressing on layers. Put bun top on sandwich and *enjoy!*

SIDE DISH RECOMMENDATIONS:

- Kroger Dill Pickles
- Kroger Fat-Free Pretzels
- Tossed Salad

SERVING SIZE & NUTRITIONAL INFORMATION:

Serving Size:
1 Sandwich

Hardy Size:
2 sandwiches

Calories: 369

Calories: 738

Total Fat: 5 g

Total Fat: 10 g

Fiber: 2 g

Fiber: 4 g

Sodium: 2480 mg

Sodium: 4960 mg

Cholesterol: 48 mg

Cholesterol: 96 mg

Carbohydrates: 43.7 g

Carbohydrates: 87.4 mg

Protein: 35 g

Protein: 70 g

Hot Crab & Cheese Delight

GROCERY LIST:

 **Brands**

Other Items:
crab meat
small white onion
small wheat pitas

INGREDIENTS:

8 ounces crab meat

½ teaspoon Kroger Lemon Juice (or juice of lemon)

2 tablespoons white onion, minced

2 tablespoons Kroger Lite Whipped Dressing

6 whole wheat small pita bread

6 Kroger Fat-Free Cheese Slices

Kroger Cocktail Sauce (optional, for dipping)

DIRECTIONS:

Put crab meat in a mixing bowl, squeeze lemon juice over it and toss. Add white onion and whipped dressing.

Lightly toast 6 pita breads (do not open bread). Spread crab mixture in even amounts on top of toasted pitas.

Place in preheated broiler for 2–3 minutes. Add 1 slice of cheese to top of each pita and broil until cheese is melted— approximately 4 minutes.

Eat and enjoy.

For added zest, dip bites into Kroger Cocktail Sauce. Delicious!

SIDE DISH RECOMMENDATIONS:

• Tossed Salad

SERVING SIZE & NUTRITIONAL INFORMATION:

Serving Size:
  1 pita

Calories: 148

Total Fat: 1.5

Fiber: 2 g

Sodium: 558 mg

Cholesterol: 34 mg

Carbohydrates: 17 g

Protein: 15 g

Hardy Size:
  2 pitas

Calories: 296

Total Fat: 3 g

Fiber: 4 g

Sodium: 1116 mg

Cholesterol: 68 mg

Carbohydrates: 34 g

Protein: 30 g

Macaroni & Cheese

GROCERY LIST:

 **Brands**

INGREDIENTS:

1 box Kroger Macaroni & Cheese Dinner

2 teaspoons Kroger Butter Sprinkles

¼ cup Kroger Fat-Free Sour Cream

¼ Kroger A/B Plus Low-Fat Milk

(salt & Kroger Pepper to taste, optional)

DIRECTIONS:

Cook macaroni according to directions on box. Instead of butter or margarine use butter sprinkles and sour cream. Instead of regular milk use A/B Plus low-fat milk.

By using substitutes for butter and milk, you're avoiding approximately 25 grams of fat.

Yields 3 1-cup servings.

SIDE DISH RECOMMENDATIONS:

- Low-fat hot dogs, cut up.
- No-Time Pick-A-Vegetable

SERVING SIZE & NUTRITIONAL INFORMATION:

Serving Size: 1 cup	Hardy Size: 1½ cups
Calories: 290	Calories: 434
Total Fat: 2.6 g	Total Fat: 3.9 g
Fiber: 2 g	Fiber: 3 g
Sodium: 967 mg	Sodium: 1450 mg
Cholesterol: 9 mg	Cholesterol: 13.5 mg
Carbohydrates: 52 g	Carbohydrates: 78.5 g
Protein: 10 g	Protein: 15.5 g

Tuna Fish Pasta Salad

GROCERY LIST:

 **Brands**

Other Items:
red pepper
cucumber
carrot
red onion

INGREDIENTS:

3 cups (dry) Kroger Macaroni Salad Rotini

1 cup Kroger Fat-Free Zesty Italian Salad Dressing

1 medium red pepper (diced)

1 medium cucumber (diced)

1 medium carrot (sliced)

½ cup red onion (finely chopped)

1 6-ounce can Kroger Solid White Tuna in Water

DIRECTIONS:

Cook rotini according to directions on box.

In a large bowl combine cut up red peppers, cucumbers, carrots and red onions. Drain can of tuna fish. Add tuna fish and salad dressing to vegetables. Mix thoroughly.

Drain pasta well and let cool slightly. Pour into bowl with other items and mix well. Refrigerate.

Best when served chilled.

Yields approximately 8 1-cup servings

SIDE DISH RECOMMENDATIONS:

- Kroger English Muffin or Roll
- Kroger Cranberry-Apple Drink

SERVING SIZE & NUTRITIONAL INFORMATION:

Serving Size: 1 cup	Hardy Size: 2 cups
Calories: 151	Calories: 302
Total Fat: 1 g	Total Fat: 2 g
Fiber: 1.9 g	Fiber: 3.8 g
Sodium: 598 mg	Sodium: 1196 mg
Cholesterol: 9.4 mg	Cholesterol: 18.8 mg
Carbohydrates: 25 g	Carbohydrates: 50 g
Protein: 9.7 g	Protein: 19.4 g

Veggie Bagel

GROCERY LIST:

 **Brands**

Other Items:
yellow squash
medium zucchini
green pepper
scallions
carrot

INGREDIENTS:

2 yellow squash (diced)

1 medium zucchini (diced)

½ green pepper (diced)

3 scallions (sliced)

1 carrot (diced)

⅛ teaspoon Kroger Garlic Powder

¼ teaspoon Kroger Black Pepper

½ cup Kroger Lite Classic Shredded Mild Cheddar Cheese

2 Kroger Egg Bagels (or assorted flavor)

2 teaspoons Kroger Grated Parmesan Cheese

Kroger Buttery Cooking Spray

DIRECTIONS:

Spray pan with cooking spray and sauté cut up squash, zucchini, green pepper, scallions and carrots.

Add garlic powder and pepper while cooking. Stir frequently.

Split 2 bagels in half. Using a knife or spoon remove middle of bagels, leaving outside of bagel intact. This makes a little moat-like area to put veggies in. Toast bagels.

After veggies are soft (approx. 8–10 minutes over medium heat), add the shredded cheese until it melts. This takes approximately 1 minute.

Divide veggies evenly and serve over toasted bagels. Sprinkle each half with 2 teaspoons parmesan cheese.

For added flavor, dip in Kroger Fat-free Buttermilk Dressing.

SERVING SIZE & NUTRITIONAL INFORMATION:

Serving Size:
  ½ veggie bagel
Calories: 178
Total Fat: 3.5 g
Fiber: 2.6 g
Sodium: 308 mg
Cholesterol: 16.25 mg
Carbohydrates: 26 g
Protein: 10 g

Hardy Size:
1 veggie bagel
Calories: 356
Total Fat: 7 g
Fiber: 5.2
Sodium: 616 mg
Cholesterol: 32.5 mg
Carbohydrates: 52.7 g
Protein: 20 g

Zesty Chicken Salad Sandwich

GROCERY LIST:

 **Brands**

Other Items:

boneless skinless chicken breasts
low-fat mayonnaise
scallions
celery

INGREDIENTS:

12 ounces 98% fat-free boneless-skinless chicken breasts

½ cup Kroger Fat-Free Zesty Italian Salad Dressing

2 tablespoon Kroger Lite Whipped Dressing

2 tablespoon low-fat mayonnaise (1 g fat/tablespoon)

1 bunch scallions chopped (approx. 2 tablespoon)

1 stalk celery chopped

8 slices Kroger Multi-Grain Bread

Kroger Dill Pickles (optional)

DIRECTIONS:

Place chicken breasts and salad dressing in skillet, cover and cook over medium/high heat until thoroughly cooked. (If cooking on a grill, marinate chicken in salad dressing for 2 hours, then grill.)

For best and quickest results dice chicken, celery, scallions and carrots in processor. If one is not available simply dice vegetables and chicken with a sharp knife.

Mix all ingredients together thoroughly. Add pepper to taste (optional).

Serve on multigrain bread. (Good fiber source)

Variations: Serve on whole grain roll or bagel.

SIDE DISH RECOMMENDATIONS:

- Kroger Pickles
- Kroger Fat-Free Pretzels
- Veggie Garden Salad

SERVING SIZE & NUTRITIONAL INFORMATION:

Serving Size:
1 sandwich

Calories: 327

Total Fat: 6.9 g

Fiber: 2.6 g

Sodium: 979.5 mg

Cholesterol: 72 mg

Carbohydrates: 31 g

Protein: 32.5 g

Hardy Size:
1 ½ sandwiches

Calories: 491

Total Fat: 10 g

Fiber: 3.9 g

Sodium: 1469 mg

Cholesterol: 108 mg

Carbohydrates: 46.5 g

Protein: 49 g

Lunch Box Snacks

For Kids of All Ages!

These snacks are for more than just lunch time. If you are hungry during the day have one of these healthy, low-fat, high-fiber snacks. This will prevent you from overeating at meal times and will also keep your metabolism revving. As you can see, many of the foods that were once forbidden to the weight-conscious person are now allowed in moderation. So keep your favorites of these snacks on hand—at home, at the office, in your briefcase—because you never know when the snack attack will strike.

Lunch Box Snacks

RAISINS

Serving Size:
  ¼ cup
Calories: 130
Total Fat: 0 g
Fiber: 2 g
Sodium: 10 mg
Cholesterol: 0 mg
Carbohydrates: 31 g
Protein: 1 g

BANANAS

Serving Size:
  1 medium banana
Calories: 105
Total Fat: .6 g
Fiber: 2.7 g
Sodium: 1 mg
Cholesterol: 0 mg
Carbohydrates: 26 g
Protein: 1 g

DEVIL'S FOOD COOKIES

Serving Size:
  2 cookies
Calories: 120
Total Fat: 1 g
Fiber: 0 g
Sodium: 80 mg
Cholesterol: 0 mg
Carbohydrates: 26 g
Protein: 1 g

The Low-Fat Kroger Cookbook

ORANGE JUICE

Serving Size:
  1 can
Calories: 90
Total Fat: 0 g
Fiber: 0 g
Sodium: 0 g
Cholesterol: 0 mg
Carbohydrates: 22 g
Protein:1 g

PRETZELS

Serving Size:
  52 stick pretzels
Calories: 120
Total Fat: 0 g
Fiber: 1 g
Sodium: 560 mg
Cholesterol: 0 mg
Carbohydrates: 24 g
Protein: 3 g

RICE CAKES

Serving Size: 6 pieces
  Mini Rice Cakes
Calories: 60
Total Fat: 1 g
Fiber: .5 g
Sodium: 0 mg
Cholesterol: 0 mg
Carbohydrates: 12 g
Protein: 1 g

Lunch Box Snacks

WAFER COOKIES

Serving Size:
 8 wafers

Calories: 100

Total Fat: 0 g

Fiber: 0 g

Sodium: 50 mg

Cholesterol: 0 mg

Carbohydrates: 23 g

Protein: <1 g

GRAPES

Serving Size:
 30 grapes

Calories: 45

Total Fat: <1 g

Fiber: 1 g

Sodium: 0 mg

Cholesterol: 0 mg

Carbohydrates: 12 g

Protein: <1 g

APPLE

Serving Size:
 1 medium apple

Calories: 81

Total Fat: .5 g

Fiber: 4 g

Sodium: 1 mg

Cholesterol: 0 mg

Carbohydrates: 21 g

Protein: <1 g

DILL PICKLE

Serving Size:
    1 whole pickle
Calories: 5
Total Fat: 0 g
Fiber: <1 g
Sodium: 220 mg
Cholesterol: 0 mg
Carbohydrates: 1 g
Protein: 0 g

FAT-FREE MUFFIN

Serving Size:
    1 98% fat-free muffin
Calories: 190 (blueberry)
Total Fat: 1 g
Fiber: 1 g
Sodium: 210 mg
Cholesterol: 0 mg
Carbohydrates: 43 g
Protein: 3 g

PEACH

Serving Size:
    1 peach
Calories: 37
Total Fat: trace
Fiber: 2 g
Sodium: 0 mg
Cholesterol: 0 mg
Carbohydrates: 10 g
Protein: <1 g

Lunch Box Snacks

SANDWICH COOKIES

Serving Size:
   3 cookies
Calories: 130
Total Fat: 3 g
Fiber: 0 g
Sodium: 100 mg
Cholesterol: 0 mg
Carbohydrates: 25 g
Protein: 1 g

WATER

Serving Size:
   As much as you want
Calories: 0
Total Fat: 0 g
Fiber: 0 g
Sodium: 0 mg
Cholesterol: 0 mg
Carbohydrates: 0 g
Protein: 0 g

CRACKERS

Serving Size:
   17 crackers
Calories: 130
Total Fat: 3 g
Fiber: 2 g
Sodium: 180 mg
Cholesterol: 0 mg
Carbohydrates: 23 g
Protein: 4 g

VEGGIES & DIP

Serving Size: 1 cup veggies
    2 T dip
Calories: 70
Total Fat: .4 g
Fiber: 4 g
Sodium: 274 mg
Cholesterol: < 5 mg
Carbohydrates: 11 g
Protein: 4 g

YOGURT

Serving Size:
    1 Kid's Pack Yogurt
Calories: 120
Total Fat: 1.5 g
Fiber: 0 g
Sodium: 65 mg
Cholesterol: 5 mg
Carbohydrates: 22 g
Protein: 3 g

PUDDING

Serving Size:
    1 pudding cup
Calories: 140
Total Fat: 0 g
Fiber: 0 g
Sodium: 135 mg
Cholesterol: 0 mg
Carbohydrates: 29 g
Protein: 6 g

Lunch Box Snacks

CRANBERRY-APPLE DRINK

Serving Size:
  1 cup
Calories: 170
Total Fat: 0 g
Fiber: 0 g
Sodium: 15 mg
Cholesterol: 0 mg
Carbohydrates: 43 g
Protein: 0 g

APPLE SAUCE

Serving Size:
  ½ cup
Calories: 90
Total Fat: 0 g
Fiber: 2 g
Sodium: 15 mg
Cholesterol: 0 mg
Carbohydrates: 23 g
Protein: 0 g

POTATO CHIPS

Serving Size:
  30 chips
Calories: 110
Total Fat: 2.5 g
Fiber: 2 g
Sodium: 200 mg
Cholesterol: 0 mg
Carbohydrates: 21 g
Protein: 3 g

...For "Kids" of All Ages

APPLE JUICE

Serving Size:
  1 cup
Calories: 120
Total Fat: 0 g
Fiber: 0 g
Sodium: 10 mg
Cholesterol: 0 mg
Carbohydrates: 28 g
Protein: 0 g

VEGETABLE JUICE

Serving Size:
  1 cup
Calories: 50
Total Fat: 0 g
Fiber: 1 g
Sodium: 650 mg
Cholesterol: 0 mg
Carbohydrates: 12 g
Protein: 1 g

LITE FRUIT COCKTAIL

Serving Size:
  ½ cup
Calories: 60
Total Fat: 0 g
Fiber: 1 g
Sodium: 10 mg
Cholesterol: 0 mg
Carbohydrates: 14 g
Protein: 0 g

Main Dish Dinners

Baked Macaroni & Cheese

GROCERY LIST:

 **Brands**

Other Items:

cornstarch, dijon mustard, minced garlic, lite salt

RECIPE INGREDIENTS:

2 cups (dry) Kroger Elbow Macaroni

1 6-oz. package Kroger Lite Classics Shredded Cheddar Cheese

2 cups Kroger Skim Delux Milk

2 tablespoons cornstarch

1 teaspoon dijon mustard

½ teaspoon lite salt

¼ teaspoon Kroger Pepper

1 tablespoon Kroger Parmesan Cheese

1 tablespoon Kroger Butter Sprinkles

½ teaspoon minced garlic

⅛ cup Kroger Seasoned Bread Crumbs

DIRECTIONS:

Cook 2 cups macaroni per instructions on box. Set aside.

Heat a nonstick sauce pan or Corningware, whisk milk and cornstarch until blended. Continue to stir and heat until mixture comes to a boil. Stir in mustard, salt, pepper, parmesan cheese, butter sprinkles and garlic. Stir 1–2 minutes.

Fold in cheese and stir until melted. Pour in macaroni and mix. Sprinkle bread crumbs on top.

Bake uncovered at 350° for 10–15 minutes until bread crumbs are brown.

Yields approximately 6 cups.

SIDE DISH RECOMMENDATIONS:

- Baked Broccoli or Creamy Peas
- Corn Bread

SERVING SIZE & NUTRITIONAL INFORMATION:

Serving Size:
  1 cup

Calories: 279

Total Fat: 5.4 g

Fiber: 1.4 g

Sodium: 443 mg

Cholesterol: 18 mg

Carbohydrates: 36.8 g

Protein: 17.2 g

Hardy Size:
  1½ cups

Calories: 418

Total Fat: 8.1 g

Fiber: 2.1 g

Sodium: 664 mg

Cholesterol: 27 mg

Carbohydrates: 55 g

Protein: 25.8 g

Baked Orange Roughy

GROCERY LIST:

 Brands

Quick, Easy &
Good for You!

Other Items:
lemons

INGREDIENTS:

16 ounces Kroger Orange Roughy Fillets

1 cup Kroger Seasoned Bread Crumbs

2 tablespoons Kroger Grated Parmesan Cheese

1 teaspoons Kroger Garlic Powder

2 lemons (for juice)

Kroger Canola Cooking Spray

DIRECTIONS:

Spray 9 x 13 inch pan with cooking spray.

In a shallow pan or large plate combine bread crumbs, parmesan cheese, and garlic. Rinse off fillets and then coat with mixture of bread crumbs on both sides of fillets. Lay fillets in 9 x 13 inch pan.

Cut lemons and squeeze juice over fillets in pan.

Bake at 375° for 20–25 minutes until thoroughly cooked.

Yields 4 4-ounce fillets.

SIDE-DISH RECOMMENDATIONS:

- Green Bean Casserole or Creamy Peas
- Cheesy Scalloped Potatoes or Twice Baked Potatoes
- Loaded Baked Potato
- Pick-a-Bread

SERVING SIZE & NUTRITIONAL INFORMATION:

Serving Size:
   4 oz. fillet

Calories: 224

Total Fat: 4 g

Fiber: 1 g

Sodium: 728.3 mg

Cholesterol: 30.4 mg

Carbohydrates: 19.7 g

Protein: 26.9 g

Hardy Size:
   8 oz. fillet

Calories: 448

Total Fat: 8 g

Fiber: 2 g

Sodium: 1456.6 mg

Cholesterol: 60.8 mg

Carbohydrates: 39.4 g

Protein: 53.8 g

Baked Shells

GROCERY LIST:

 **Brands**

Great for Parties!

RECIPE INGREDIENTS:

- 1 16-ounce box of Kroger Salad Shells
- 2 jars Kroger Spaghetti Sauce
- 1 package Kroger Lite Classics Shredded Mozzarella Cheese
- 1 15-ounce container of Kroger Fat-Free Ricotta Cheese
- ½ teaspoon Kroger Garlic Powder
- 2 tablespoons Kroger Grated Parmesan Cheese
- Kroger Canola Cooking Spray

DIRECTIONS:

Fill large sauce pan with water and bring to a boil. Pour box of salad shells into boiling water and cook for 9–11 minutes stirring frequently. Drain when done and return to large sauce pan.

Add spaghetti sauce, mozzarella cheese, ricotta cheese, and garlic powder to cooked noodles in pan. Stir thoroughly.

Spray 9 x 13 inch baking dish with non-stick spray and pour shell mixture into pan and spread evenly.

Sprinkle parmesan cheese on top and cover loosely with foil. Bake at 350° for 35–40 minutes until heated. Yields approximately 10 1-cup servings. (Make ahead of time and refrigerate until ready to bake.)

SIDE DISH RECOMMENDATIONS:

- Veggie Garden Salad
- Skinny Garlic Bread

SERVING SIZE & NUTRITIONAL INFORMATION:

Serving Size:
  1 cup

Calories: 316

Total Fat: 4.5

Fiber: 4.4 g

Sodium: 1419 mg

Cholesterol: 24.5 mg

Carbohydrates: 49.7 g

Protein: 18 g

Hardy Size:
  2 cups

Calories: 632

Total Fat: 9 g

Fiber: 8.8 g

Sodium: 2838 mg

Cholesterol: 49 mg

Carbohydrates: 99.4 g

Protein: 36 g

Cheese Manicotti

GROCERY LIST:

 **Brands**

Other Items:
manicotti pasta
minced garlic

RECIPE INGREDIENTS:

8 ounces manicotti pasta

1 container (15 ounces) Kroger Fat-Free Ricotta Cheese

¼ cup Kroger Break-Free or Kroger Egg Substitute

1 cup Kroger Lite Classics Shredded Mozzarella Cheese

¼ cup Kroger Grated Parmesan Cheese

¼ teaspoon Kroger Pepper

½ teaspoon minced garlic

2 cups Kroger Mushroom Spaghetti Sauce

Kroger Canola Cooking Spray

DIRECTIONS:

Cook 8 ounces of manicotti pasta according to directions on box. Rinse with cold water and drain.

In the meantime, combine ricotta cheese, egg substitute, ¾ cup mozzarella cheese, ⅛ cup parmesan cheese, pepper, and garlic. Mix well.

Spray a 9 x 13 inch baking dish with non-stick cooking spray. Using a dull knife, stuff manicotti shells with cheese mixture and place stuffed shells side by side in a single layer in baking dish.

Pour spaghetti sauce over shells and sprinkle with remaining mozzarella and parmesan cheese. Bake at 350° for 30–35 minutes. Yields 4 servings.

SIDE DISH RECOMMENDATIONS:

- Tomato & Zucchini Salad
- Skinny Garlic Bread

SERVING SIZE & NUTRITIONAL INFORMATION:

Serving Size:
   3 pieces

Calories: 454

Total Fat: 7.4 g

Fiber: 4 g

Sodium: 1338 mg

Cholesterol: 57.5 mg

Carbohydrates: 56 g

Protein: 37 g

Hardy Size:
   4 pieces

Calories: 606

Total Fat: 9.8 g

Fiber: 5 g

Sodium: 1784 mg

Cholesterol: 77 mg

Carbohydrates: 75 g

Protein: 49 g

Chicken Parmesan

GROCERY LIST:

 **Brands**

Other Items:
boneless breasts of chicken

RECIPE INGREDIENTS:

4 6-ounce boneless, skinless chicken breasts (1½ pounds)

½ cup Kroger Seasoned Bread Crumbs

1 tablespoon Kroger Grated Parmesan Cheese

½ teaspoon Kroger Garlic Powder

1 jar Kroger Mushroom Spaghetti Sauce

4 slices Kroger Lite Classics Mozzarella Cheese

Kroger Canola Cooking Spray

DIRECTIONS:

In a shallow pan or large plate combine bread crumbs, parmesan cheese, and garlic powder.

Wash chicken breasts and remove any visible fat. While still wet, roll each breast in bread crumb mixture. Place breaded breasts side by side in a 9 x 13 inch baking dish sprayed with non-stick spray.

Pour jar of mushroom spaghetti sauce evenly over breasts. Place a slice of cheese over each breast. Cover pan with foil.

Bake at 375° for 25 minutes with foil on. Then remove foil and bake for 20 more minutes or until chicken is completely done. (To reduce fat even more, leave cheese off.)

SIDE DISH RECOMMENDATIONS:

- Skinny Garlic Bread
- Veggie Garden Salad or Cucumber & Scallion Salad
- Cheesy Scalloped Potatoes

SERVING SIZE & NUTRITIONAL INFORMATION:

Serving Size: ½ Chicken Breast (3 ozs.)

Calories: 255

Total Fat: 6.8 g

Fiber: 2 g

Sodium: 1093 mg

Cholesterol: 80 mg

Carbohydrates: 13.5 g

Protein: 32.6 g

Hardy Size: 1 Chicken Breast (6 ozs.)

Calories: 510

Total Fat: 13.6 g

Fiber: 4 g

Sodium: 2186 mg

Cholesterol: 160 mg

Carbohydrates: 27 g

Protein: 65.2 g

Chicken with Stuffing & Gravy

GROCERY LIST:

 Brands

Other Items:

boneless, skinless chicken breasts
98% fat-free cream of chicken soup

INGREDIENTS:

1 pound boneless, skinless chicken breasts

1 6-ounce box Kroger Stuffing Magic

1 can 98% fat-free cream of chicken soup

1 can (2 cups) Kroger Chicken Broth

½ cup water

Kroger Canola Cooking Spray

Kroger Aluminum Foil

DIRECTIONS:

Spray a 13 x 9 inch baking dish with cooking spray. Pour dry package of stuffing into pan. Add seasoning packet and mix thoroughly. Add can of chicken broth, water, and can of cream of chicken soup. Mix thoroughly.

Wash boneless breast of chicken and place in mixture. (Wash hands and surfaces after handling chicken.) Spread a little of mixture on top of chicken so it won't dry out while baking. Cover with foil.

Bake in oven for 45 minutes at 350°. Remove foil and bake for 10 minutes more.

One pan and no mess!

SIDE DISH RECOMMENDATIONS:

- Mashed Potato Casserole or Wild Rice with Broccoli
- Cucumber & Scallion Salad
- Pick-a-Bread

SERVING SIZE & NUTRITIONAL INFORMATION:

Serving Size:
  4 oz. breast & 1 cup
  stuffing & gravy

Calories: 420

Total Fat: 9.6 g

Fiber: 1.5 g

Sodium: 1542 mg

Cholesterol: 108 mg

Carbohydrates: 37.5 g

Protein: 43 g

Hardy Size:
  6 oz. breast & 1½ cup
  stuffing & gravy

Calories: 631

Total Fat: 14.4 g

Fiber: 2.3 g

Sodium: 2319 mg

Cholesterol: 162.2 g

Carbohydrates: 56.4 g

Protein: 65.2 g

Chili Macaroni

GROCERY LIST:

 **Brands**

Other Items:
low-fat ground turkey
chili seasoning

RECIPE INGREDIENTS:

1 pound low-fat ground turkey
1 package chili seasoning
½ cup water
1 15-ounce can Kroger Tomato Sauce
1 can Kroger Chili Hot Beans in Chili Gravy
½ box (2 cups uncooked) Kroger Elbow Macaroni
Kroger Fat Free Sour Cream (2 tablespoons per serving)
Kroger Lite Classics Shredded Cheese (2 tablespoons
   per serving)

DIRECTIONS:

In large sauce pan brown ground turkey. Drain fat. Stir in chili seasoning, water, tomato sauce, and chili beans. Let simmer.

In another sauce pan prepare elbow macaroni according to directions on box using ½ of the box. Drain macaroni when done.

Add drained macaroni to chili pan and stir thoroughly.

Yields approximately 6 1-cup servings.

Top each serving with 2 tablespoons sour cream and ⅛ cup shredded lite cheese.

Great for leftovers too!

SIDE DISH RECOMMENDATIONS:

- Carrots with Caraway Seeds
- No-Time Pick-A-Vegetable
- Corn Bread

SERVING SIZE & NUTRITIONAL INFORMATION:

Serving Size:
  1 cup

Calories: 408

Total Fat: 9 g

Fiber: 5 g

Sodium: 1043 mg

Cholesterol: 79 mg

Carbohydrates: 51 g

Protein: 31 g

Hardy Size:
  1 ½ cups

Calories: 612

Total Fat: 13.6 g

Fiber: 7.5 g

Sodium: 1565 mg

Cholesterol: 119 mg

Carbohydrates: 77 g

Protein: 47 g

Mexican Lasagna

GROCERY LIST:

 **Brands**

Other Items:

ground lean beef or turkey
onion
low-fat cream of mushroom soup
taco mix
fat-free flour tortilla shells

RECIPE INGREDIENTS:

1 pound ground turkey or lean beef

½ cup chopped onion

1 package taco mix

2 cans low-fat cream of mushroom soup

1 16-ounce jar Kroger Picante Sauce

1 cup Kroger Fat-Free Sour Cream

6 fat-free tortilla shells

1 6-ounce package Kroger Lite Classics Shredded Cheddar
Cheese

Kroger Canola Cooking Spray

DIRECTIONS:

Brown meat and add chopped onion. Add taco mix seasoning and ¾ cup water. Set aside. In mixing bowl combine following: mushroom soup, picante sauce, and sour cream. In 13 x 9 inch pan spray non-stick cooking spray.

Now the layering of the lasagna begins. Put approximately ½ cup of sauce mixture in bottom of pan and spread evenly. Place 2 taco shells side by side on top of it. Then add a layer of the taco meat, and cover with approximately ⅓ of sauce. Layer another 2 shells, then taco meat, then ⅓ of sauce. Layer another 2 shells then meat and remaining sauce. On top layer after sauce, sprinkle with cheese. Bake at 350° for 35–40 minutes until thoroughly heated and cheese on top is melted.

SIDE DISH RECOMMENDATIONS:

- Herb & Butter Rice
- Low-fat Tortilla Chips with Kroger Picante Sauce
- Corn with Mustard Sauce

SERVING SIZE & NUTRITIONAL INFORMATION:

Serving Size:
⅛ of recipe

Calories: 332

Total Fat: 9 g

Fiber: 1.7 g

Sodium: 1540 mg

Cholesterol: 72.5 mg

Carbohydrates: 38 g

Protein: 21.4 g

Hardy Size:
⅙ of recipe

Calories: 443

Total Fat: 12 g

Fiber: 2.4 g

Sodium: 2053 mg

Cholesterol: 97 mg

Carbohydrates: 50 g

Protein: 28.5 g

Sloppy Joes

GROCERY LIST:

 **Brands**

Other Items:
1 lb. ground turkey
or lean beef

INGREDIENTS:

1 pound ground turkey or lean beef

1 cup Kroger Ketchup

3 tablespoon Kroger Light Brown Sugar

1 tablespoon Kroger White Vinegar

2 tablespoon Kroger Worcestershire Sauce

Kroger Canola Cooking Spray

1 package (8-count) Kroger Wheat Sandwich Buns

Kroger Dill Pickles (optional)

DIRECTIONS:

Spray frying pan with cooking spray. Brown meat. Add ketchup, vinegar, brown sugar, and worcestershire sauce.

Heat thoroughly.

Serve on sandwich buns with pickles.

Easy, Easy, Easy!

SIDE DISH RECOMMENDATIONS:

- Kroger Low-Fat Macaroni or Potato Salad (Kroger Deli)
- Baked Beans

SERVING SIZE & NUTRITIONAL INFORMATION:

Serving Size: 1 Sandwich	Hardy Size: 2 Sandwiches
Calories: 265	Calories: 530
Total Fat: 5.9	Total Fat: 11.8 g
Fiber: <1 g	Fiber: <2 g
Sodium: 666 mg	Sodium: 1332
Cholesterol: 50 mg	Cholesterol: 100 mg
Carbohydrates: 36.3 g	Carbohydrates: 72.6 g
Protein: 17.6 g	Protein: 35.2 g

Spaghetti Stir Fry

GROCERY LIST:

 **Brands**

INGREDIENTS:

8 ounces Kroger Angel Hair Pasta

1 16-ounce bag Kroger Stir Fry Vegetable Blend

Kroger Vegetable Oil Cooking Spray

2 tablespoons Kroger Soy Sauce

½ cup water

¼ teaspoon Kroger Garlic Powder

⅛ teaspoon Kroger Ginger

DIRECTIONS:

Cook pasta according to directions on box. Do the same with the vegetables, substituting cooking spray for oil.

In a serving dish combine pasta and vegetables. Combine water and soy sauce, garlic, and ginger. Pour over pasta and vegetables.

Mix thoroughly.

Yields approximately 4 2-cup servings.

SIDE DISH RECOMMENDATIONS:

- Veggie Garden Salad
- Cheese-filled Zucchini Boats

SERVING SIZE & NUTRITIONAL INFORMATION:

Serving Size:
2 cups

Calories: 255 g

Total Fat: 1 g

Fiber: 4.5

Sodium: 619 mg

Cholesterol: 0

Carbohydrates: 50.5 g

Protein: 10.5 g

Hardy Size:
3 cups

Calories: 383

Total Fat: 1.5 g

Fiber: 6.8 g

Sodium: 930 mg

Cholesterol: 0

Carbohydrates: 76 g

Protein: 15.8 g

Tortellini & Sauce

GROCERY LIST:

 **Brands:**

Easy & Quick Recipe!

RECIPE INGREDIENTS:

1 package Kroger Tortellini (with beef)

1 jar of Kroger Mushroom Spaghetti Sauce

½ teaspoon Kroger Italian Seasoning (to taste)

Approximately 3 tablespoons Kroger Grated Parmesan Cheese
(2 teaspoons per serving)

DIRECTIONS:

Prepare tortellini as directed on package.

In another pan heat up spaghetti sauce and add Italian seasoning to taste.

After tortellini is drained add it to sauce. Top with grated parmesan cheese (optional).

Makes approximately 4 ¾-cup servings

SIDE-DISH RECOMMENDATIONS:

- Appetizer: Garlic Pizza Spread
- Tomato & Zucchini Salad
- Pick-a-Bread

SERVING SIZE & NUTRITIONAL INFORMATION:

Serving Size: ¾ cup
  with parmesan cheese

Calories: 331

Total Fat: 9 g

Fiber: 4.4 g

Sodium: 2148 mg

Cholesterol: 27 mg

Carbohydrates: 52.5 g

Protein: 12.5 g

Hardy Size: 1½ cups
  with cheese

Calories: 662

Total Fat: 18 g

Fiber: 8.8 g

Sodium: 4296 mg

Cholesterol: 54 mg

Carbohydrates: 105 g

Protein: 25 g

Side Dishes:
Vegetables

Baked Beans

 **Brands**

RECIPE INGREDIENTS:

2 21-ounce cans of Kroger Baked Beans

2 tablespoons Kroger Light Brown Sugar

1 tablespoons Kroger Worcestershire Sauce

3 tablespoons Kroger Tomato Ketchup

1 teaspoon Kroger Mustard

DIRECTIONS:

In 2-quart casserole combine all ingredients. Mix thoroughly.

Bake at 350° for 30–35 minutes until hot throughout.

Makes approximately 10 ½-cup servings.

High in Fiber, Low in Fat!

SERVING SIZE & NUTRITIONAL INFORMATION:

Serving Size:
  ½ cup

Calories: 145

Total Fat: 1 g

Fiber: 6 g

Sodium: 524 mg

Cholesterol: 0

Carbohydrates: 27 g

Protein: 7 g

Hardy Size:
  1 cup

Calories: 290

Total Fat: 2 g

Fiber: 12 g

Sodium: 1048

Cholesterol: 0

Carbohydrates: 54 g

Protein: 14 g

Baked Broccoli

GROCERY LIST:

 **Brands**

Other Items:
bunch of broccoli

RECIPE INGREDIENTS:

2 ½ cups broccoli crowns

¼ Kroger Grated Parmesan Cheese

1 cup Kroger Seasoned Bread Crumbs

½ cup Kroger Egg Substitute

Kroger Buttery Cooking Spray

Kroger Fat-Free Buttermilk Dressing (optional, for dipping)

The Low-Fat Kroger Cookbook

DIRECTIONS:

Wash and cut broccoli crowns. Cook in boiling water until tender yet firm. (You may steam instead if desired.) Let cool.

In shallow pan or plate combine parmesan cheese and bread crumbs.

Dip broccoli crowns into egg substitute and then roll in bread crumb mixture.

Place in a baking dish that has been lined with foil and sprayed with cooking spray. Bake at 350° for 20 minutes. Yields 5 ½-cup servings.

For added flavor dip in Kroger Fat-Free Buttermilk Dressing.

SERVING SIZE & NUTRITIONAL INFORMATION:

Serving Size:
  ½ cup
Calories: 146
Total Fat: 3.2 g
Fiber: 2.1 g
Sodium: 628 mg
Cholesterol: 6 mg
Carbohydrates: 18.3 g
Protein: 9.7 g

Hardy Size:
  1 cup
Calories: 292
Total Fat: 6.4 g
Fiber: 4.2 g
Sodium: 1256 mg
Cholesterol: 12 mg
Carbohydrates: 36.6 g
Protein: 19.4 g

Carrots with Caraway Seeds

GROCERY LIST:

 **Brands**

INGREDIENTS:

1 20-ounce bag Kroger Frozen Fresh Crinkle Cut Carrots

1 tablespoon Kroger Butter Sprinkles

¼ teaspoon Kroger Dried Parsley Flakes

1 teaspoon Kroger Caraway Seeds

DIRECTIONS:

Steam, boil, or microwave carrots until tender.

Drain water and immediately add butter sprinkles, parsley, and caraway seeds. Mix thoroughly.

Yields 7 ⅔-cup servings

SERVING SIZE & NUTRITIONAL INFORMATION:

Serving Size:	Hardy Size:
⅔ cup	1 ⅓ cup
Calories: 39.5	Calories: 79
Total Fat: 0	Total Fat: < 1 g
Fiber: 2.1 g	Fiber: 4.2 g
Sodium: 105 mg	Sodium: 210 mg
Cholesterol: 0	Cholesterol: 0
Carbohydrates: 6 g	Carbohydrates: 12 g
Protein: 1 g	Protein: 2 g

Cheese-Filled Zucchini Boats

GROCERY LIST:

 **Brands**

Other Items:
zucchini

RECIPE INGREDIENTS:

3 medium zucchini

½ cup Kroger Lite Classics Shredded Cheddar Cheese

½ cup Kroger Fat-Free Ricotta Cheese

¼ cup Kroger Break-Free or Kroger Egg Substitute

1 tablespoon Kroger Parsley

¼ cup Kroger Bread Crumbs

Kroger Buttery Cooking Spray

DIRECTIONS:

Cut zucchini in halves lengthwise. Steam zucchini 8–10 minutes until just tender. Scoop out center of zucchini to make a cradle. Set aside.

In bowl combine cheddar cheese, ricotta cheese, egg substitute, and parsley. Stir thoroughly.

Take mixture and fill in hollowed-out zucchini boats using up all the mixture. Distribute evenly. Sprinkle each boat with bread crumbs.

Spray baking dish with cooking spray and place zucchini boats in dish. Bake at 350° for 20 minutes.

Yields 6 zucchini boats.

SERVING SIZE & NUTRITIONAL INFORMATION:

Serving Size:
  1 boat

Calories: 74

Total Fat: 1.7 g

Fiber: .7

Sodium: 185 mg

Cholesterol: 12 mg

Carbohydrates: 6.3 g

Protein: 7.8 g

Hardy Size:
  2 boats

Calories: 148

Total Fat: 3.4 g

Fiber: 1.4 g

Sodium: 370 mg

Cholesterol: 24 mg

Carbohydrates: 12.6 g

Protein: 15.6 g

Corn with Mustard Sauce

GROCERY LIST:

 **Brands**

Other Items:
sweet red (or green) pepper
sweet onion
Dijon mustard

RECIPE INGREDIENTS:

1 16-ounce package Kroger Frozen Whole Kernel Corn

1 medium sweet red pepper (diced)

3 tablespoons chopped onion

¼ cup water

2 teaspoons Kroger Butter Sprinkles

4 teaspoons Dijon mustard

⅛ teaspoon Kroger Pepper

DIRECTIONS:

In 1-quart microwaveable casserole dish combine corn, peppers, onion, and water. Cover and cook 7–8 minutes.

Add butter sprinkles, mustard, and pepper. Stir, cover, and cook 1–2 more minutes, until vegetables are tender.

Makes 6 ½-cup servings.

SERVING SIZE & NUTRITIONAL INFORMATION:

Serving Size:
  ½ cup
Calories: 85.5
Total Fat: 1.5 g
Fiber: 1.3 g
Sodium: 138 mg
Cholesterol: 0
Carbohydrates: 19 g
Protein: 3 g

Hardy Size:
  1 cup
Calories: 171
Total Fat: 3 g
Fiber: 2.6 g
Sodium: 276 mg
Cholesterol: 0
Carbohydrates: 38 g
Protein: 6 g

Creamy Peas

GROCERY LIST:

 **Brands**

RECIPE INGREDIENTS:

2 cups or 1 10-ounce package Kroger Frozen Peas

1 tablespoon water

¼ cup Kroger Skim Delux Milk

¼ cup Kroger Fat-Free Cream Cheese

⅛ teaspoon Kroger Pepper

⅛ teaspoon Kroger Garlic Powder

1½ teaspoons Kroger Butter Sprinkles

DIRECTIONS:

In a medium casserole dish combine peas and water.

Cover and cook in microwave 8–10 minutes until peas are tender. Drain.

Stir in milk, cream cheese, pepper, garlic powder, and butter sprinkles. Mix well, re-cover and microwave for approximately 3 minutes.

Makes 4 ½-cup servings.

SERVING SIZE & NUTRITIONAL INFORMATION:

Serving Size: ½ cup	Hardy Size: 1 cup
Calories: 76	Calories: 152
Total Fat: .6 g	Total Fat: 1.2 g
Fiber: 3 g	Fiber: 6 g
Sodium: 194 mg	Sodium: 388 mg
Cholesterol: 3 mg	Cholesterol: 6 mg
Carbohydrates: 12 g	Carbohydrates: 24 g
Protein: 6 g	Protein: 12 g

Cucumber & Scallion Salad

GROCERY LIST:

 **Brands**

Other Items:
cucumber
scallions
lite salt

RECIPE INGREDIENTS:

1 ½ cups sliced cucumber

¼ cup scallions, finely chopped

⅛ teaspoon lite salt

1 teaspoon Kroger Parmesan Cheese

¼ teaspoon Kroger Hot Sauce

Dash of Kroger Pepper

½ cup Kroger Fat-Free Sour Cream

DIRECTIONS:

Slice cucumber thinly. Add finely chopped scallions, salt, parmesan cheese, hot sauce, and pepper.

Add sour cream and mix thoroughly.

Best when chilled before serving.

Yields 4 servings (½ cup each)

This recipe is so good, it will bring tears to your eyes!

SERVING SIZE & NUTRITIONAL INFORMATION:

Serving Size:
  ½ cup
Calories: 37
Total Fat: .3 g
Fiber: .5 g
Sodium: 93 mg
Cholesterol: 6 mg
Carbohydrates: 7 g
Protein: 1.6 g

Hardy Size:
  1 cup
Calories: 74
Total Fat: .6 g
Fiber: <1 g
Sodium: 186 mg
Cholesterol: 12 mg
Carbohydrates: 14 g
Protein: 3 g

Green Bean Casserole

GROCERY LIST:

 Brands

Other Items:
98% fat-free cream of mushroom soup

RECIPE INGREDIENTS:

2 9-ounce boxes Kroger French Style Sliced Green Beans

1 can 98% fat-free cream of mushroom soup

1 tablespoon Kroger Salad Magic Country Style Buttermilk
Dressing

¼ cup Kroger Seasoned Bread Crumbs

Kroger Buttery Cooking Spray

DIRECTIONS:

In mixing bowl thaw beans. (Suggestion: thaw in microwave.) Drain excess water.

Combine and thoroughly mix green beans, cream of mushroom soup, and salad magic dressing mix.

Spray either 9 x 9 inch baking dish or 1 ½ quart casserole with non-stick buttery spray.

Put bean mix in dish, sprinkle with bread crumbs, and bake at 350° for 30 minutes.

Makes approximately 6 servings ¾ cup each.

Always a hit for covered dish parties!

SERVING SIZE & NUTRITIONAL INFORMATION:

Serving Size: ¾ cup	Hardy Size: 1 ½ cups
Calories: 82.5	Calories: 165
Total Fat: 1.3 g	Total Fat: 2.6 g
Fiber: 3 g	Fiber: 6 g
Sodium: 453 mg	Sodium: 906 mg
Cholesterol: 4 mg	Cholesterol: 8 mg
Carbohydrates: 14 g	Carbohydrates: 28 g
Protein: 2 g	Protein: 4 g

Tomato, Zucchini & Feta Salad

GROCERY LIST:

 **Brands**

Other Items:
tomatoes
zucchini
scallions
feta cheese

INGREDIENTS:

2 large tomatoes (cut into wedges)

2 medium zucchini (sliced)

¼ cup scallions (sliced)

½ teaspoon Kroger Basil (crushed)

¼ cup Kroger Fat-Free Zesty Italian Salad Dressing

3 tablespoon (1 ½ oz.) feta cheese

DIRECTIONS:

In a bowl combine tomato, zucchini, scallions, basil, and salad dressing.

Add feta cheese just before serving.

Serves 4.

Try this easy recipe for your next cookout!

SERVING SIZE & NUTRITIONAL INFORMATION:

Serving Size:
  ¼ recipe

Calories: 49.5

Total Fat: 2.5 g

Fiber: .7 g

Sodium: 375 mg

Cholesterol: 9.4 mg

Carbohydrates: 3.8 g

Protein: 2.2 g

Hardy Size:
  ½ recipe

Calories: 99

Total Fat: 5 g

Fiber: 1.4 g

Sodium: 750 mg

Cholesterol: 18.8 mg

Carbohydrates: 7.6 g

Protein: 4.4 g

Vegetable & Cheese Casserole

GROCERY LIST:

 Brands

Other Items:
98% fat-free cream of mushroom soup

RECIPE INGREDIENTS:

1 16-ounce package of Kroger Frozen Fresh Mixed Vegetables

1 can 98% fat-free cream of mushroom soup

½ cup Kroger Lite Classics Shredded Mild Cheddar Cheese

⅛ teaspoon Kroger Garlic Powder

¼ cup Kroger Seasoned Bread Crumbs

Kroger Buttery Cooking Spray

Dash of Kroger pepper (optional)

DIRECTIONS:

Spray 9 x 9 inch baking dish with cooking spray.

In a bowl combine vegetables, cream of mushroom soup, cheese, garlic, and pepper. Mix thoroughly.

Spread mixture evenly in baking dish. Sprinkle bread crumbs over top.

Bake at 350° for 30–35 minutes, until heated thoroughly.

Yields approximately 10 ½-cup servings.

Vegetables are loaded with vitamins.

SERVING SIZE & NUTRITIONAL INFORMATION:

Serving Size:
  ½ cup

Calories: 74.5

Total Fat: 1.8 g

Fiber: 1.6 g

Sodium: 236 mg

Cholesterol: 5.5 mg

Carbohydrates: 10.4 g

Protein: 4 g

Hardy Size:
  1 cup

Calories: 149

Total Fat: 3.6 g

Fiber: 3.2 g

Sodium: 472 mg

Cholesterol: 11 mg

Carbohydrates: 21 mg

Protein: 8 g

Veggie Garden Salad

Hardy knows green salads are good for you!

Serving Size: Load up!

Make sure you use fat-free or low-fat dressings.

spinach lettuce	celery	zucchini
romaine lettuce	onions	green pepper
red leaf lettuce	cauliflower	red pepper
broccoli	squash	snow peas, etc.
carrots	red beets	

DIRECTIONS:

Pick several of the vegetables listed, cut up for a fresh salad, and choose one of Kroger's fat-free dressing.

High in fiber and vitamins!

No-Time Pick-A-Vegetable

GROCERY LIST:

 **Brands**

Serving Size: ½ to ⅔ cup

Calories: 25 to 80

Fat: 0 to 1 g

Fiber: 1 to 5 g

Cholesterol: 0 mg

Sodium: 10 to 140 mg

(See each pkg. for exact amount)

DIRECTIONS:

Pick one of the above and steam, boil, or microwave according to directions on bag. Sprinkle with butter sprinkles, lite salt, pepper, or any of your favorite spices.

Low in sodium, high in vitamins!

Side Dishes:
Rice & Potatoes

Buttery New Potatoes

GROCERY LIST:

 **Brands**

Other Items:

new potatoes

INGREDIENTS:

10 small new potatoes

1 tablespoon Kroger Butter Sprinkles

1 teaspoon Kroger Parsley Flakes

2 teaspoons Kroger Parmesan Cheese

¼ teaspoon Kroger Pepper

DIRECTIONS:

Fill a 2½-quart saucepan three-fourths full of water and bring to a boil. Add new potatoes and boil approximately 20 minutes or until potatoes are tender. (The smaller the potato the quicker it cooks.)

Drain water and cut potatoes into quarters (wedges). While still hot, transfer potatoes into a covered dish. Add butter sprinkles, parsley flakes, parmesan cheese, and pepper. Cover. Hold dish and lid and shake gently until ingredients are mixed well.

Make 4 servings.

SERVING SIZE & NUTRITIONAL INFORMATION:

Serving Size:
 ¼ of recipe

Calories: 163

Total Fat: .4 g

Fiber: 2.5 g

Sodium: 137 mg

Cholesterol: 1.25 mg

Carbohydrates: 34 g

Protein: 2 g

Hardy Size:
 ½ of recipe

Calories: 326

Total Fat: .8 g

Fiber: 5 g

Sodium: 274 mg

Cholesterol: 2.5 mg

Carbohydrates: 68 g

Protein: 4 g

Cheesy Scalloped Potatoes

GROCERY LIST:

 **Brands**

Other Items:
medium potatoes
minced garlic

INGREDIENTS:

4 medium potatoes (peeled and sliced)

2½ cups Kroger A/B Plus Low-Fat Milk

2 tablespoons Kroger Flour

1 tablespoon Kroger Butter Sprinkles

¼ teaspoon minced garlic

⅛ teaspoon Kroger Pepper

1 tablespoon Kroger Instant Minced Onion

1 cup Kroger Lite Classics Shredded Cheddar Cheese

½ cup Kroger Fat-Free Ricotta Cheese

Kroger Canola Cooking Spray

DIRECTIONS:

To make sauce, mix milk, flour, butter sprinkles, garlic, and pepper in a sauce pan over medium heat until mixture thickens. Stir continuously. Add cheese and onion.

Spray a medium casserole dish with cooking spray. Place half of the sliced potatoes in dish. Cover with half of the sauce and half of the cheddar cheese. Add remaining potatoes, then rest of sauce and cheddar cheese.

Bake at 350° for approximately 70 minutes, stirring occasionally.

Yields approximately 6 ¾-cup servings.

SERVING SIZE & NUTRITIONAL INFORMATION:

Serving Size:
¾ cup

Calories: 188.5

Total Fat: 3.3 g

Fiber: 1.5 g

Sodium: 249 mg

Cholesterol: 18.8 mg

Carbohydrates: 24 g

Protein: 14 g

Hardy Size:
1 ½ cups

Calories: 377

Total Fat: 6.6 g

Fiber: 3 g

Sodium: 498 mg

Cholesterol: 37.6 mg

Carbohydrates: 48 g

Protein: 28 g

Herb & Butter Brown Rice

GROCERY LIST:

 Brands

INGREDIENTS:

2 cups Kroger Instant Whole Grain Rice

1 teaspoon Kroger Butter Sprinkles

1 teaspoon Kroger Garlic Powder

1 teaspoon Kroger Italian Seasoning

Kroger Pepper to taste

DIRECTIONS:

Follow directions on back of rice box to make 4 servings.

When rice is cooked add butter sprinkles, garlic powder, Italian seasoning, and pepper while still hot.

Makes 4 ½-cup servings.

SERVING SIZE & NUTRITIONAL INFORMATION:

Serving Size:
  ½ cup
Calories: 157
Total Fat: 1 g
Fiber: 2.2 g
Sodium: 41 mg
Cholesterol: 0
Carbohydrates: 34 g
Protein: 4.2 g

Hardy Size:
  1 cup
Calories: 314
Total Fat: 2 g
Fiber: 4.3 g
Sodium: 82 mg
Cholesterol: 0
Carbohydrates: 68 g
Protein: 8.4 g

Kroger Low-Fat Deli Side Choices

AMERICAN POTATO SALAD

Serving Size:
⅔ cup potato salad

Calories: 100

Total Fat: 1 g

Fiber: 3 g

Sodium: 730 mg

Cholesterol: 0 mg

Carbohydrates: 19 g

Protein: 3 g

COLE SLAW

Serving Size:
½ cup cole slaw

Calories: 80

Total Fat: .5 g

Fiber: 2 g

Sodium: 490 mg

Cholesterol: 0 mg

Carbohydrates: 17 g

Protein: 2 g

MACARONI SALAD

Serving Size:
⅔ cup macaroni salad

Calories: 140

Total Fat: 1.5 g

Fiber: 4 g

Sodium: 850 mg

Cholesterol: 0 mg

Carbohydrates: 28 g

Protein: 4 g

Kroger Low-Fat Deli Side Choices

3-BEAN SALAD

Serving Size:
⅓ cup 3-bean salad

Calories: 80

Total Fat: 0 g

Fiber: 1 g

Sodium: 470 mg

Cholesterol: 0 mg

Carbohydrates: 19 g

Protein: 1 g

Great side dishes for all those summer barbecues!

Loaded Baked Potato

GROCERY LIST:

 **Brands**

INGREDIENTS:

1 medium potato per person

Toppings to load:

Kroger Fat-Free Sour Cream

Kroger Fat-Free Wild Ranch Dip

Kroger Lite Classics Shredded Cheddar Cheese

Kroger Bac' N Buds

Kroger Butter Sprinkles

DIRECTIONS:

Bake potato at 400° for 60 minutes or until just tender. To save time, microwave approximately 10 minutes. Choose from the variety of toppings listed in the ingredients.

Great for barbecues or for a meal.

SERVING SIZE & NUTRITIONAL INFORMATION:

Serving Size:
1 medium potato
(see labels on toppings)

Calories: 220

Total Fat: .2 g

Fiber: 4.8 g

Sodium: 16 mg

Cholesterol: 0

Carbohydrates: 51 g

Protein: 4.7 g

Low in fat and a good source of carbohydrates, potatoes make a filling lunch as well as a great side to most main dishes.

Mashed Potato Casserole

GROCERY LIST:

 **Brands**

Other Items:
potatoes

INGREDIENTS:

2½ pounds potatoes

1 cup Kroger Fat-Free Cream Cheese

½ cup Kroger Fat-Free Sour Cream

4 teaspoons Kroger Onion Soup & Dip Mix

2 teaspoons Kroger Parsley

DIRECTIONS:

Peel and quarter potatoes. Boil until tender (approximately 30 minutes). Drain. With mixer or food processor, mash potatoes. Slowly add cream cheese, sour cream, onion dip, and pepper. Mixture should be fluffy.

Spoon into casserole dish and cover. Bake in a 350° preheated oven for approximately 45 minutes.

Yields approximately 8 ¾-cup servings.

Suggestion: To save time, use Kroger Instant Potatoes.

SERVING SIZE & NUTRITIONAL INFORMATION:

Serving Size:
  approx. ¾ cup

Calories: 129

Total Fat: < .1 g

Fiber: 1.7 g

Sodium: 231 mg

Cholesterol: 7.5 mg

Carbohydrates: 25 g

Protein: 6.7 g

Hardy Size:
  approx. 1½ cups

Calories: 258

Total Fat: < .2 g

Fiber: 3.4 g

Sodium: 462 mg

Cholesterol: 15 mg

Carbohydrates: 50 g

Protein: 13.4 g

Twice Baked Potatoes

GROCERY LIST:

 **Brands**

Other Items:
medium potatoes
lite salt

INGREDIENTS:

3 medium potatoes

1 cup Kroger Lite Classics Shredded Cheddar Cheese

1 cup Kroger Fat-Free Sour Cream

1 tablespoon Kroger Butter Sprinkles

¼ teaspoon Kroger Basil

⅛ teaspoon lite salt

2 tablespoons Kroger Chives

2 tablespoons Kroger A/B Plus Low-Fat Milk

1 teaspoon Kroger Paprika

1 tablespoon Kroger Grated Parmesan Cheese

DIRECTIONS:

Bake potatoes in oven at 375° for 50–55 minutes or until tender. Let potatoes cool for 10 minutes or so. Cut potatoes in half lengthwise and scoop out pulp, leaving potato skin shell.

In a mixing bowl, combine scooped out potato, cheese, sour cream, butter sprinkles, basil, salt, and chives. While mixing, slowly add milk. Beat until mixture has right consistency. Place skins on baking sheet. Spoon mixture evenly into potato skins. Sprinkle paprika and parmesan cheese on top. Cover loosely with foil.

Bake at 375° for 12 minutes covered. Remove foil and bake for 8–10 minutes uncovered.

Yields 6 twice baked potato halves.

Goes great with most any main dish meal!

SERVING SIZE & NUTRITIONAL INFORMATION:

Serving Size:
  1 potato skin

Calories: 210

Total Fat: 3.2 g

Fiber: 2.5 g

Sodium: 267 mg

Cholesterol: 18 mg

Carbohydrates: 33 g

Protein: 10 g

Hardy Size:
  2 potato skins

Calories: 420

Total Fat: 6.4 g

Fiber: 5 g

Sodium: 534 mg

Cholesterol: 36 mg

Carbohydrates: 66 g

Protein: 20 g

Wild Rice with Broccoli

GROCERY LIST:

 **Brands**

INGREDIENTS:

6 ounces Kroger Long Grain Wild Rice

2 ½ cups Kroger Frozen Fresh Chopped Broccoli

1 cup Kroger Chicken Broth

1 cup Kroger Lite Classics Shredded Cheddar Cheese

2 tablespoons Kroger Seasoned Bread Crumbs

DIRECTIONS:

To prepare rice, make these modifications from the box directions: In a sauce pan, combine 2½ cups of water (leave out margarine), rice and seasoning packet. Stir. Bring to a boil, cover, reduce heat and simmer for 20 minutes.

Add frozen broccoli and continue to simmer for 5 more minutes. Add chicken broth and cheese. Stir until mixed well.

Pour into medium casserole and sprinkle with bread crumbs. Cover and bake at 350° for 35 minutes. For last 10 minutes remove cover.

Yields 8 ½-cup servings.

SERVING SIZE & NUTRITIONAL INFORMATION:

Serving Size:
  ½ cup
Calories: 137
Total Fat: 2.3 g
Fiber: 1.7 g
Sodium: 547.5 mg
Cholesterol: 8.1 mg
Carbohydrates: 18.7 g
Protein: 7.8 g

Hardy Size:
  1 cup
Calories: 274
Total Fat: 4.6 g
Fiber: 3.4 g
Sodium: 1095 mg
Cholesterol: 16.2 mg
Carbohydrates: 37.4 g
Protein: 15.6 g

Side Dishes:
Breads

Bacon and Cheese Muffins

GROCERY LIST:

 **Brands**

Kroger Brands
save you plenty!

RECIPE INGREDIENTS:

4 Kroger Wheat English Muffins

½ cup Kroger Lite Classics Shredded Cheddar Cheese

4 teaspoon Kroger Bac'N Buds

DIRECTIONS:

Split muffins. Add 1 tablespoon of shredded cheese and ½ teaspoon of Bac'N Buds to each half.

Place on cookie sheet and bake in 350° preheated oven for approximately 10–12 minutes until cheese is melted.

SERVING SIZE & NUTRITIONAL INFORMATION:

Serving Size:
   1 muffin half

Calories: 90

Total Fat: 1.6 g

Fiber: 1.5 g

Sodium: 178.3 mg

Cholesterol: 3.75 mg

Carbohydrates: 13.3 g

Protein: 5.75 g

Hardy Size:
   2 muffin halves

Calories: 180

Total Fat: 3.2 g

Fiber: 3 g

Sodium: 356.6 mg

Cholesterol: 7.5 mg

Carbohydrates: 26.6 g

Protein: 11.5 g

Corn Bread

GROCERY LIST:

 **Brands**

Other Items:
baking powder
lite salt

INGREDIENTS:

¼ cup Break-Free or Kroger Egg Substitute

1 cup Kroger A/B Plus Low-Fat Milk

1 tablespoon Kroger Apple Sauce

1 cup Kroger Flour

¾ cup Kroger Cornmeal

1 tablespoon Kroger Sugar

1 tablespoon baking powder

½ teaspoon lite salt

Kroger Canola Cooking Spray

DIRECTIONS:

In a medium mixing bowl combine egg substitute, milk, and apple sauce until blended well. Stir in flour, cornmeal, sugar, baking powder, and salt.

Spray a 9 x 9 inch baking pan with cooking spray. Pour mixture into pan and bake for approximately 20 minutes at 400°.

Makes 12 pieces.

SERVING SIZE & NUTRITIONAL INFORMATION:

Serving Size:
  1 piece
Calories: 83.5
Total Fat: .4 g
Fiber: 1 g
Sodium: 286 mg
Cholesterol: <1 mg
Carbohydrates: 17 g
Protein: 2.8 g

Hardy Size:
  2 pieces
Calories: 167
Total Fat: .8 g
Fiber: 2 g
Sodium: 572 mg
Cholesterol: <2 mg
Carbohydrates: 34 g
Protein: 5.6 g

Skinny Garlic Bread

GROCERY LIST:

 **Brands**

Other Items:
minced garlic
8-oz french bread

INGREDIENTS:

1 8-ounce loaf or 2 4-ounce loaves french bread
(from the Deli)

1 tablespoon Kroger Fat-Free Zesty Italian Dressing

1 tablespoon minced garlic

4 teaspoon Kroger Grated Parmesan Cheese

2 teaspoon Kroger Butter Sprinkles

Kroger Aluminum Foil

DIRECTIONS:

In a small mixing bowl combine salad dressing, garlic, parmesan cheese, and butter sprinkles.

Cut loaf lengthwise and spread mixture onto both halves. Put loaf back together and wrap in foil. Bake in preheated oven at 350° for 10–15 minutes.

Cut into 2-inch segments. Best when served immediately.

Each 8-ounce loaf makes approximately 10 slices.

SERVING SIZE & NUTRITIONAL INFORMATION:

Serving Size:
  1 slice

Calories: 70

Total Fat: 1.4 g

Fiber: .5 g

Sodium: 194 mg

Cholesterol: 1 mg

Carbohydrates: 11 g

Protein: 2.8 g

Hardy Size:
  2 slices

Calories: 140

Total Fat: 2.8 g

Fiber: 1 g

Sodium: 388 mg

Cholesterol: 2 mg

Carbohydrates: 22 g

Protein: 5.6 g

Pick-a-Bread

 **Brands**

BROWN & SERVE BUTTERMILK ROLLS

Serving Size: 1 Roll
Calories: 80
Fat: 1.5 g
Fiber: 0
Cholesterol: 0
Sodium: 140 mg

BUTTERMILK BISCUITS

Serving Size: 2 biscuits
Calories: 100
Fat: 1.5 g
Fiber: 1g
Cholesterol: 0
Sodium: 360 mg

DINNER ROLLS (From the Deli)

Serving Size: 1 Roll
Calories: 90
Fat: 1 g
Fiber: 1 g
Cholesterol: 0
Sodium: 170 mg

DIRECTIONS:

Follow directions on package. Quick and easy to prepare.
Low in fat, high in satisfaction.

Appetizers

Celery & Cream Cheese

GROCERY LIST:

 **Brands**

Other Items:
celery
scallions

INGREDIENTS:

6 celery stalks

½ cup Kroger Fat-Free Cream Cheese

2 tablespoon scallions (finely chopped)

2 teaspoon Kroger Grated Parmesan Cheese

DIRECTIONS:

Wash and trim edges of celery sticks.

In a food processor or with mixer thoroughly combine cream cheese, scallions, and parmesan.

Using a knife, spread mixture into celery groove. Cut each celery stalk into thirds.

Yields 18 cheese-filled celery sticks.

MAIN DISH RECOMMENDATIONS:

Goes with everything!

SERVING SIZE & NUTRITIONAL INFORMATION:

Serving Size:
   3 celery sticks

Calories: 31

Total Fat: .4 g

Fiber: .75 g

Sodium: 152 mg

Cholesterol: 4.2 mg

Carbohydrates: 3.6 g

Protein: 3.3 g

Hardy Size:
   6 celery sticks

Calories: 62

Total Fat: .8 g

Fiber: 1.5 g

Sodium: 304 mg

Cholesterol: 8.4 mg

Carbohydrates: 7.2 g

Protein: 6.6 g

Cheese & Crackers

GROCERY LIST:

 **Brands**

INGREDIENTS:

1 box Sensible Indulgence Wheat Squares

1 ounce Kroger Lite Classics Colby Cheese

1 ounce Kroger Lite Classics Monterey Jack Cheese

1 ounce Kroger Lite Classics Sharp Cheddar Cheese

DIRECTIONS:

Pick out your favorite cheese. Cut into slices.

Arrange on a serving plate with crackers.

Good when time is short and the guests are starting to arrive.

Quick & Easy
To Prepare for Your
Next Party!

MAIN DISH RECOMMENDATIONS:

Great for any type of main dish!

SERVING SIZE & NUTRITIONAL INFORMATION:

Serving Size: 10 crackers, 1 oz. of cheese

Calories: 157

Total Fat: 5.8 g

Fiber: 1.2 g

Sodium: 286 mg

Cholesterol: 15 mg

Carbohydrates: 13.6 g

Protein: 11.4 g

Hardy Size: 20 crackers, 2 oz. of cheese

Calories: 314 g

Total Fat: 11.6 g

Fiber: 2.4 g

Sodium: 572 mg

Cholesterol: 30 mg

Carbohydrates: 27.2 g

Protein: 22.8g

Chilled Mexican Layer Dip

GROCERY LIST:

 **Brands**

Other Items:
taco seasoning mix
medium tomato
scallions

RECIPE INGREDIENTS:

1 can Kroger Fat-Free Refried Beans

½ cup Kroger Picante Sauce (Mild or Medium)

1 tablespoon taco seasoning mix (any brand)

1 cup Kroger Fat-Free Sour Cream

1 cup Kroger Lite Classics Shredded Cheddar Cheese

1 medium tomato (diced)

¼ cup scallions (sliced)

10 whole Kroger Black Olives (sliced)

DIRECTIONS:

In mixing bowl combine refried beans, picante sauce and 1 tablespoon of taco seasoning mix. Mix thoroughly.

Pour above mixture into a 9 x 9 inch baking dish (or a casserole dish approximately the same size). Spread evenly across bottom of pan.

Layer on top of bean mixture in the following order: Sour cream, cheese, diced tomatoes, chopped scallions, and then olives.

Serve chilled with low-fat tortilla chips for dipping.

Great for summer barbeques or parties!

SERVING SIZE & NUTRITIONAL INFORMATION:

Serving Size:
 ⅛ of appetizer

Calories: 130

Total Fat: 2.4 g

Fiber: 3.8 g

Sodium: 674 mg

Cholesterol: 6.7 mg

Carbohydrates: 17 g

Protein: 8 g

Hardy Size:
 ⅙ of appetizer

Calories: 196

Total Fat: 3.6 g

Fiber: 5.8 g

Sodium: 1012 mg

Cholesterol: 10 mg

Carbohydrates: 26 g

Protein: 12 g

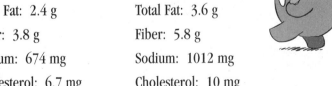

Creamy Zucchini Rounds

GROCERY LIST:

 **Brands**

Other Items:
zucchini
low-fat mayonnaise

RECIPE INGREDIENTS:

½ cup low-fat mayonnaise (1 gram of fat per tablespoon)

½ cup Kroger Grated Parmesan Cheese

½ teaspoon Kroger Basil (crushed)

2 medium zucchinis

Kroger Canola Cooking Spray

DIRECTIONS:

Preheat broiler.

In a bowl combine mayonnaise, parmesan cheese, and basil.

Cut zucchini into ¼ inch round slices.

Lightly spray cookie sheet. Spread a thin layer of mixture on top of each zucchini round and place side by side on cookie sheet.

Broil approximately 1–2 minutes or until lightly brown.

Best when served immediately.

Yields approximately 40 zucchini rounds.

MAIN DISH RECOMMENDATIONS:

- Baked Macaroni & Cheese
- Baked Orange Roughy
- Baked Shells

SERVING SIZE & NUTRITIONAL INFORMATION:

Serving Size:
    5 zucchini rounds

Calories: 67

Total Fat: 3.3 g

Fiber: .4 g

Sodium: 291 mg

Cholesterol: 7.5 mg

Carbohydrates: 5 g

Protein: 3.4 g

Hardy Size:
    10 zucchini rounds

Calories: 134.5

Total Fat: 6.6 g

Fiber: .8 g

Sodium: 582

Cholesterol: 15 mg

Carbohydrates: 10 g

Protein: 6.8 g

Frijoles Fiesta Dip

GROCERY LIST:

 **Brands**

Other Items:
green chilies
scallions

RECIPE INGREDIENTS:

1 16-ounce can Kroger Fat-Free Refried Beans

4 tablespoons green chilies (chopped)

½ teaspoon Kroger Hot Sauce

½ cup Kroger Fat-Free Sour Cream

1 cup Kroger Lite Classics Shredded Sharp Cheddar Cheese

2 tablespoons Kroger Picante Sauce

2 tablespoons scallions (chopped)

DIRECTIONS:

In a medium sized bowl combine refried beans, green chilies, and hot sauce. Pour mixture into a one quart casserole dish and spread evenly.

Spread sour cream evenly on top of mixture. Mix cheese and picante sauce together and spread on top of sour cream.

Bake in preheated oven at 350° until cheese is melted, approximately 15–20 minutes. Once baked, top with sliced scallions.

This recipe can easily be multiplied for large parties.

Recommended for dipping: Low-fat tortilla chips or cut up soft flour tortillas.

MAIN DISH RECOMMENDATIONS:

• Mexican Lasagna

SERVING SIZE & NUTRITIONAL INFORMATION:

Serving Size:
  ⅛ of recipe

Calories: 110.5

Total Fat: 2 g

Fiber: 3.6 g

Sodium: 420 mg

Cholesterol: 10 mg

Carbohydrates: 13 g

Protein: 8.5 g

Hardy Size:
  ⅙ of recipe

Calories: 147

Total Fat: 2.7 g

Fiber: 4.8 g

Sodium: 560 mg

Cholesterol: 13 mg

Carbohydrates: 17 g

Protein: 11 g

Garlic Pizza Spread

GROCERY LIST:

 **Brands**

RECIPE INGREDIENTS:

1 cup Kroger Fat-Free Cream Cheese

¼ cup Kroger Lite Classic Shredded Mozzarella Cheese

½ cup Kroger Mushroom Spaghetti Sauce

1 teaspoon Kroger Garlic Powder

8 Kroger Large Pitted Olives (sliced)

DIRECTIONS:

Preheat oven to 350°. Spread cream cheese on bottom of 9-inch pie plate. Top with half of the shredded mozzarella, then sauce. Sprinkle garlic powder on top of sauce and cover with the the other half of shredded cheese. Sprinkle sliced olives on top.

Bake until cheese is melted and mixture is warmed thoroughly (approximately 20 minutes).

Serve warm with cut up French bread or crackers.

·*Other suggested toppings:* onions, green or red peppers, jalapeno peppers, mushrooms, etc.

MAIN DISH RECOMMENDATIONS:

- Cheese Manicotti
- Tortellini & Sauce
- Chicken Parmesan

SERVING SIZE & NUTRITIONAL INFORMATION:

Serving Size:
 ⅙ of recipe

Calories: 69.5

Total Fat: 1.5 g

Fiber: .3 g

Sodium: 417 mg

Cholesterol: 9 mg

Carbohydrates: 6 g

Protein: 7 g

Hardy Size:
 ¼ of recipe

Calories: 104

Total Fat: 2.3 g

Fiber: .5 g

Sodium: 626 mg

Cholesterol: 14 mg

Carbohydrates: 9 g

Protein: 10 g

Hot Cheese & Chili Bean Dip

GROCERY LIST:

 **Brands**

Easy, Delicious & High in Fiber!

RECIPE INGREDIENTS:

2 15½-ounce cans Kroger Chili Hot Beans in Chili Gravy
1 cup Kroger Lite Classics Shredded Cheddar Cheese
Kroger Canola Cooking Spray

DIRECTIONS:

Spray 9 x 9 inch baking dish with cooking spray.

Open beans and drain the juice from one can. Empty both cans of beans (and juice of one) into baking dish.

Sprinkle the shredded cheese over top evenly.

Bake at 350° for approximately 20 minutes or until cheese is melted.

Serve warm with a bowl of low-fat tortilla chips.

MAIN DISH RECOMMENDATIONS:

• Chili Macaroni

SERVING SIZE & NUTRITIONAL INFORMATION:

Serving Size:
    ⅙ of recipe
Calories: 163
Total Fat: 4 g
Fiber: 5 g
Sodium: 577 mg
Cholesterol: 10 mg
Carbohydrates: 18 g
Protein: 12 g

Hardy Size:
    ¼ of recipe
Calories: 245
Total Fat: 6.2 g
Fiber: 7.5 g
Sodium: 865 mg
Cholesterol: 15 mg
Carbohydrates: 27 g
Protein: 18 g

Spicy Artichoke Dip

GROCERY LIST:

 **Brands**

Other Items:
artichoke hearts
green chilis

RECIPE INGREDIENTS:

6 artichoke hearts (8½-ounce can)

½ cup green chilies

2 tablespoons Kroger Lite Whipped Dressing

1 cup Kroger Lite Classics Shredded Sharp Cheddar Cheese

1 teaspoon Kroger Hot Sauce

DIRECTIONS:

Using a food processor or blender pureé artichoke hearts and green chilies. Add mayonnaise, cheese, and hot sauce.

Pour mixture into baking dish. Cover and bake at 350° for 15–20 minutes. Remove cover and bake for 5 minutes longer.

Suggestion: Use between ¼ and ½ cup green chilies depending on spicy preference.

Use low-fat tortilla chips or low-fat crackers for dipping.

Hot, Spicy & Delicious!

SERVING SIZE & NUTRITIONAL INFORMATION:

Serving Size:	Hardy Size:
⅙ of recipe	¼ of recipe
Calories: 85	Calories: 127.5
Total Fat: 3.7 g	Total Fat: 5.5 g
Fiber: 1.7 g	Fiber: 2.5 g
Sodium: 363 mg	Sodium: 545 mg
Cholesterol: 10 mg	Cholesterol: 15 mg
Carbohydrates: 5 g	Carbohydrates: 7 g
Protein: 7 g	Protein: 10.5 g

Spinach Dip

GROCERY LIST:

 **Brands**

Other Items:
Mayonnaise

Always a hit
at parties!

RECIPE INGREDIENTS:

1 12-ounce package Kroger Fresh Frozen Chopped Spinach

2 tablespoon Kroger Grated Parmesan Cheese

2 tablespoon Kroger Salad Magic Buttermilk Salad
Dressing Mix

¾ cup low-fat mayonnaise (1 gram fat per tablespoon)

DIRECTIONS:

Thaw box of chopped spinach and drain excess water.

In mixing bowl combine spinach, parmesan cheese, butter-milk dressing mix, and low-fat mayonnaise.

Mix thoroughly, place in serving dish and refrigerate.

Best if served chilled. Serve with low-fat crackers or Kroger Mixed Deli Rolls cut into bite-sized pieces.

Yields 2 cups.

MAIN DISH RECOMMENDATIONS:

Goes With Most Any Main Dish!

SERVING SIZE & NUTRITIONAL INFORMATION:

Serving Size:
 ¼ cup

Calories: 63

Total Fat: 2 g

Fiber: .9 g

Sodium: 523 mg

Cholesterol: 2 mg

Carbohydrates: 2.4 g

Protein: 1.6 g

Hardy Size:
 ½ cup

Calories: 126

Total Fat: 4 g

Fiber: 1.8 g

Sodium: 1046 mg

Cholesterol: 4 mg

Carbohydrates: 4.8 g

Protein: 3.2 g

Sweet Onion Dip

GROCERY LIST:

 **Brands**

Other Items:

large Vidalia Onion (sweet)
low-fat mayonnaise

INGREDIENTS:

1 cup sweet onion (finely chopped)

1 cup low-fat mayonnaise (1 gram fat per tablespoon)

1 cup Kroger Lite Classics Shredded Mild Cheddar Cheese

Kroger Canola Cooking Spray

Kroger Sensible Indulgence Wheat Crackers

DIRECTIONS:

In a medium bowl combine onions, mayonnaise, and shredded cheese. Mix thoroughly.

Spray small baking dish with cooking spray and pour mixture in. Bake at 350° for approximately 20 minutes.

If Vidalia Onions are not in season use any sweet onion.

Serve warm with low-fat wheat crackers.

Yields 8 ⅓-cup servings.

MAIN DISH RECOMMENDATIONS:

A good appetizer for any dish.

SERVING SIZE & NUTRITIONAL INFORMATION:

Serving Size:
⅓ cup dip (see box for crackers)

Calories: 98

Total Fat: 4 g

Fiber: .4 g

Sodium: 361 mg

Cholesterol: 7.5 mg

Carbohydrates: 9.7 g

Protein: 4.7 g

Hardy Size:
½ cup dip (see box for crackers)

Calories: 130

Total Fat: 5 g

Fiber: .5 g

Sodium: 481 mg

Cholesterol: 10 mg

Carbohydrates: 13 g

Protein: 6.3 g

Desserts

Chocolate Crème de Cacao Cheesecake

GROCERY LIST:

 **Brands**

Other Items:
crème de cacao liqueur
mini chocolate chips
lite salt

RECIPE INGREDIENTS:

6 Kroger Chocolate Graham Crackers
1 cup Kroger Sugar
1 ½ cups Kroger Fat-Free Cream Cheese
1 cup Kroger Fat-Free Cottage Cheese
¼ cup Kroger Flour
6 tablespoon Kroger Unsweetened Cocoa
¼ cup crème de cacao liqueur
1 teaspoon Kroger Vanilla
¼ teaspoon lite salt
½ cup Kroger Break-Free or Kroger Egg Substitute
2 tablespoon mini chocolate chips
Kroger Canola Cooking spray

DIRECTIONS:

In a large bowl, using a mixer (or food processor) blend sugar, cream cheese, cottage cheese, flour, cocoa, crème de cacao, vanilla, and salt.

Fold in egg substitute until smooth. Sprinkle chocolate chips over mixture and stir into batter.

Spray thoroughly a 7-inch spring form pan, bottom and sides, with cooking spray.

Finely crush graham crackers and press into bottom of the pan. Pour mixture over crushed graham crackers.

In 300° preheated oven, bake for 65–70 minutes. If using an 8-inch pan bake for 40–45 minutes.

Variations: Substitute crème de menthe or amaretto for crème de cacao.

SERVING SIZE & NUTRITIONAL INFORMATION:

Serving Size: Cut into 10ths / 1 piece

Calories: 214.8

Total Fat: 1.9 g

Fiber: 1 g

Sodium: 335 mg

Cholesterol: 8 mg

Carbohydrates: 35.9 g

Protein: 10 g

Hardy Size: Cut into 8ths / 1 piece

Calories: 268.5

Total Fat: 2.3 g

Fiber: 1.3 g

Sodium: 419 mg

Cholesterol: 10 mg

Carbohydrates: 45 g

Protein: 12.5 g

Fudge Brownie Deluxe

GROCERY LIST:

 **Brands**

RECIPE INGREDIENTS:

1 box Kroger Fudge Brownie Deluxe Mix

¼ cup Kroger Apple Sauce

¼ cup Kroger Egg Substitute

Kroger Buttery Cooking Spray

DIRECTIONS:

Follow directions on box using these modifications:

Use apple sauce instead of oil.

Use egg substitute instead of egg.

Spray baking pan with cooking spray.

SERVING SIZE & NUTRITIONAL INFORMATION:

Serving Size:
  $\frac{1}{20}$ of mix

Calories: 24

Total Fat: 2.5 g

Fiber: 1 g

Sodium: 109.8 mg

Cholesterol: 0

Carbohydrates: 25 g

Protein: 1.3 g

Hardy Size:
  $\frac{1}{10}$ of mix

Calories: 48

Total Fat: 5 g

Fiber: 2 g

Sodium: 219.6 mg

Cholesterol: 0

Carbohydrates: 50 g

Protein: 2.6 g

Ice Cream Extravaganza

GROCERY LIST:

 **Brands**

RECIPE INGREDIENTS:

Your Choice:

½ cup vanilla or chocolate Kroger Low-Fat Frozen Yogurt
   or Kroger Healthy Indulgence Low-Fat Ice Cream

2 tablespoons of one of the above toppings

Optional: Kroger Sprinkles (1 teaspoon is 1 gram of fat)

DIRECTIONS:

Scoop up frozen yogurt or ice cream into bowls and add your favorite topping.

Ice cream is a treat any day of the year!

SERVING SIZE & NUTRITIONAL INFORMATION:

Serving Size:
  ½ cup low-fat yogurt &
  2 T topping

Calories: 230

Total Fat: 2.5 g

Fiber: 0

Sodium: 75 mg

Cholesterol: 10 mg

Carbohydrates: 48 g

Protein: 3 g

Hardy Size:
  1 cup low-fat yogurt &
  4 T topping

Calories: 460

Total Fat: 5 g

Fiber: 0

Sodium: 150 mg

Cholesterol: 20 mg

Carbohydrates: 96 g

Protein: 6 g

* *Nutritional amounts may vary (only slightly) depending on topping choice. See specific labels.*

No Nut Banana Bread

GROCERY LIST:

 **Brands**

Other Items:
baking powder
bananas
lite salt

RECIPE INGREDIENTS:

1½ cups Kroger Flour

½ teaspoon Kroger Baking Soda

1¼ teaspoon baking powder

½ teaspoon Kroger Nutmeg

⅛ teaspoon lite salt

1 cup mashed bananas

¼ package Kroger Egg Substitute

¾ cup Kroger Sugar

¼ cup Kroger Apple Sauce

Kroger Buttery Cooking Spray

DIRECTIONS:

In a large mixing bowl combine mashed bananas, egg substitute, sugar, and apple sauce. Mix well.

In a small bowl combine flour, baking soda, baking powder, nutmeg, and salt. Add to banana mixture and mix thoroughly.

Spray bread pan generously with cooking spray. Pour batter into pan. Bake at 350° for 45–50 minutes.

Cut into 12 slices.

SERVING SIZE & NUTRITIONAL INFORMATION:

Serving Size:
  1 slice

Calories: 124

Total Fat: .1 g

Fiber: 1 g

Sodium: 88.4 mg

Cholesterol: 0

Carbohydrates: 29.3 g

Protein: 2.2 g

Hardy Size:
  2 slices

Calories: 248

Total Fat: .2 g

Fiber: 2 g

Sodium: 176.8 mg

Cholesterol: 0

Carbohydrates: 58.6 g

Protein: 4.4 g

Sweet Strawberry Angel Food Cake

GROCERY LIST:

 Brands

Other Items:
   angel food cake (bakery)

RECIPE INGREDIENTS:

   1 Angel Food Cake (from Kroger bakery)
   1 bag or box Kroger Frozen Sliced Strawberries
   ¼ cup Kroger Confectioner's Sugar

DIRECTIONS:

Sprinkle 2 tablespoons confectioner's sugar on top of cake. Pour ½ of the thawed strawberries on top of cake, letting juice drizzle down sides.

In a small bowl combine rest of powdered sugar and strawberries. Set aside until ready to serve.

Cut cake and add approximately 2 tablespoons of set-aside strawberries over each slice.

Variation: Top with Kroger Low-Fat Whipped Cream or Kroger Low-Fat Frozen Vanilla Yogurt.

A Heavenly Fat-Free Dessert!

SERVING SIZE & NUTRITIONAL INFORMATION:

Serving Size:
  ⅛ of cake with
  strawberry topping

Calories: 186

Total Fat: 0

Fiber: 1 g

Sodium: 160 mg

Cholesterol: 0

Carbohydrates: 44 g

Protein: .4 g

Hardy Size:
  2 slices with strawberry
  topping

Calories: 372

Total Fat: 0

Fiber: 2 g

Sodium: 320 mg

Cholesterol: 0

Carbohydrates: 88 g

Protein: .8 g

240

42-Oz. Pkg.
Butter or Butter Light

Kroger
Microwave Popcorn

60¢ OFF
WITH COUPON

LIMIT ONE COUPON PER CUSTOMER.

241

15-Oz. Ctn.

Kroger
Seedless Raisins

55¢ OFF
WITH COUPON

LIMIT ONE COUPON PER CUSTOMER.

LIMIT ONE COUPON PER CUSTOMER.

AVAILABLE ONLY IN STORES WITH A PHARMACY.
EXCLUDES INSURANCE CO-PAYMENTS,
THIRD PARTY PLANS, AND TRANSFERS FROM ANOTHER KROGER.

$2 OFF
WITH COUPON

ANY NEW OR TRANSFERRED*
PHARMACY
PRESCRIPTION

*On transferred prescriptions in the state of South Carolina, our Pharmacist will
contact your doctor for a new prescription. Coupon not to be doubled.
Not good in conjunction with any other offer.

LIMIT ONE COUPON PER CUSTOMER.

AVAILABLE ONLY IN STORES WITH A PHARMACY.
EXCLUDES INSURANCE CO-PAYMENTS,
THIRD PARTY PLANS, AND TRANSFERS FROM ANOTHER KROGER.

$2 OFF
WITH COUPON

ANY NEW OR TRANSFERRED*
PHARMACY
PRESCRIPTION

*On transferred prescriptions in the state of South Carolina, our Pharmacist will
contact your doctor for a new prescription. Coupon not to be doubled.
Not good in conjunction with any other offer.

In The Pastry Shoppe

275

TRY OUR "FAT FREE"

18-Oz. Pkg.

Angel Food Cake

30¢ OFF

WITH COUPON

Pumpkin Pie Spice

AMERICA'S BRAND
Kroger
QUALITY GUARANTEED

60¢ OFF
Kroger Spice
Any Size, Any Flavor

Accounting Dept. Forward To:
The Kroger Co., Div. 049, 1014 Vine Street, Cincinnati, OH 45202
Subject to State and Local Taxes. Void where prohibited by law.

5 11110 65160 5

COCONUT

AMERICA'S BRAND
Kroger
QUALITY GUARANTEED

60¢ OFF
Kroger Coconut
One 14 Oz. Bag

Accounting Dept. Forward To:
The Kroger Co., Div. 049, 1014 Vine Street, Cincinnati, OH 45202
Subject to State and Local Taxes. Void where prohibited by law.

5 11110 95860 5

LIGHT CORN SYRUP

AMERICA'S BRAND
Kroger
QUALITY GUARANTEED

60¢ OFF
Kroger Light Corn Syrup
One 32 Oz. Bottle

Accounting Dept. Forward To:
The Kroger Co., Div. 049, 1014 Vine Street, Cincinnati, OH 45202
Subject to State and Local Taxes. Void where prohibited by law.

5 11110 66360 8

60¢ OFF
Kroger Baking Extract
One 1 Oz. Bottle

Accounting Dept. Forward To:
The Kroger Co., Div. 049, 1014 Vine Street, Cincinnati, OH 45202
Subject to State and Local Taxes. Void where prohibited by law.

5 11110 60560 8

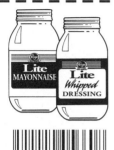

60¢ OFF
Kroger Lite Mayonnaise or
Lite Whipped Salad Dressing
One 32 Oz. Jar

Accounting Dept. Forward To:
The Kroger Co., Div. 049, 1014 Vine Street, Cincinnati, OH 45202
Subject to State and Local Taxes. Void where prohibited by law.

5 11110 05660 8

60¢ OFF 2
Kroger Shredded Cheese
8 Oz. Bags
(must purchase 2 to receive 60¢ off)

Accounting Dept. Forward To:
The Kroger Co., Div. 049, 1014 Vine Street, Cincinnati, OH 45202
Subject to State and Local Taxes. Void where prohibited by law.

5 11110 91331 4

60¢ OFF
Kroger Lite
Nice'n Cheesy
One 2 Lb. Loaf

Accounting Dept. Forward To:
The Kroger Co., Div. 049, 1014 Vine Street, Cincinnati, OH 45202
Subject to State and Local Taxes. Void where prohibited by law.

5 11110 90160 1

AMERICA'S BRAND
Kroger
QUALITY GUARANTEED

60¢ OFF
Kroger Reduced Fat
Creamy Peanut Butter Spread
One 18 Oz. Jar

Accounting Dept. Forward To:
The Kroger Co., Div. 049, 1014 Vine Street, Cincinnati, OH 45202
Subject to State and Local Taxes. Void where prohibited by law.

5 11110 92260 6

AMERICA'S BRAND
Kroger
QUALITY GUARANTEED

60¢ OFF 2
Kroger Gelatin and Puddings
.3 to 3.0 Oz. Box
(must purchase 2 to receive 60¢ off)

Accounting Dept. Forward To:
The Kroger Co., Div. 049, 1014 Vine Street, Cincinnati, OH 45202
Subject to State and Local Taxes. Void where prohibited by law.

5 11110 61931 5

AMERICA'S BRAND
Kroger
QUALITY GUARANTEED

60¢ OFF
Kroger Fat Free
Pourable Salad Dressing
One 24 Oz. Bottle

Accounting Dept. Forward To:
The Kroger Co., Div. 049, 1014 Vine Street, Cincinnati, OH 45202
Subject to State and Local Taxes. Void where prohibited by law.

5 11110 05860 2

404756 | MANUFACTURER COUPON | NO EXPIRATION | 404756

Save 65¢
on one package of
HEALTHY CHOICE®
Franks or Smoked Sausage

RETAILER: Please redeem for face value as specified. ANY OTHER USE CONSTITUTES FRAUD. You will be paid face value plus 8¢ for handling, provided you and your customer complied with the terms of this offer and invoices showing purchases sufficient to cover coupons are shown on request. Send coupons to: Armour Swift-Eckrich, CMS Department #27000, One Fawcett Drive, Del Rio, TX 78840. NOT TO BE SOLD, NON-REPRODUCIBLE. Customer must pay any sales tax. VOID WHERE TAXED, RESTRICTED OR PROHIBITED. Cash redemption value of 1/20 of one cent. Limit one coupon per purchase. ©1996 ARMOUR SWIFT-ECKRICH.

5 50100 60065 0